# Perm

## The Secret Life and Legacy of Barack Hussein Obama

**By Cliff Kincaid, Constance Cumbey,
Peter LaBarbera, and Tina Trent**

"What I learned, in searching for missing kids around the world, is that those of us who are driven for the truth, as you are, in exposing those dark corners of the world, you have got to keep plugging away. You can't take 'no' for an answer and you can't back off because they say 'that's impossible' or 'that couldn't be.' The information you have uncovered has been extraordinarily helpful in having us understand the New World Order – what the forces of evil are actually trying to do to take over freedom and democracy. Except for your work, we wouldn't know any of this."

- Child advocate Elizabeth Yore, speaking to Cliff Kincaid on America's Survival TV, February 14, 2017, about our Soros Files project.

## America's Survival, Inc.

America's Survival, Inc. (ASI) operates a global television channel, maintains several websites, distributes regular reports and columns, and offers a free smartphone app for the public to get ASI news and information. Our Internet-based YouTube and Roku channel, America's Survival TV, is produced in association with broadcaster Jerry Kenney.

ASI obtained and released the 600-page FBI file on Frank Marshall Davis, Obama's communist mentor, who was suspected of conducting espionage for the Soviet Union. ASI held a November 10, 2017, National Press Club conference on Russia-gate, looking at the evidence that it was the Obama Administration which had been working with Russia, and that Obama was the real Russian agent.

Our books, *Comrade Obama Unmasked* and *Red Star Rising,* make the case that Obama was a security risk who couldn't pass a background check and whose presidency aided America's enemies in the communist and Muslim worlds. Under Obama, major security lapses and intelligence failures took place. Our books tell the story of how Obama came to power and was protected in office by Deep State operatives in the U.S. intelligence community who were then enlisted in a campaign against President Donald J. Trump.

**Author Bios:**

America's Survival Inc. (ASI) President **Cliff Kincaid** is a veteran journalist and media critic who concentrated in journalism and communications at the University of Toledo, where he graduated with a Bachelor of Arts degree. At his college newspaper, Cliff won an award for editorial writing from the Society of Professional Journalists and came to Washington through a national journalism program headed by conservative author and journalist M. Stanton Evans. Hired out of college by Accuracy in Media (AIM) founder Reed Irvine, Cliff served as editor of the AIM Report and director of the Accuracy in Media Center for Investigative Reporting. Cliff served on the staff of *Human Events* for several years and was an editorial writer and newsletter editor for former National Security Council staffer Oliver North at his Freedom Alliance educational foundation. Cliff appears in a Newseum film on media bias and anonymous sources.

Cliff is the author or co-author of several books, including *Global Bondage: The U.N. Plan to Rule the World, Global Taxes for World Government, Blood on His Hands: The True Story of Edward Snowden, Back from the Dead: The Return of the Evil Empire, Red Jihad, The Sword of Revolution and the Communist Apocalypse*, *Marxist Madrassas, Comrade Obama Unmasked: Marxist Mole in the White House*, and *Red Star Rising: The Making of Barack Hussein Obama and the Transformation of America.*

**Constance Cumbey** is a Michigan attorney who wrote the first major book critical of the New Age Movement, the best-selling *The Hidden Dangers of the Rainbow* (Huntington House, 1983). She pioneered the work against the New Age Movement from a Christian perspective. There are best-selling German, Norwegian, and Dutch editions of her book. She has practiced law in Michigan since 1975 and has been listed in Who's Who in the World, Who's Who in America, and Who's Who in American Law. Her papers and work have been archived by the University of Michigan's Bentley Historical Library at its invitation and request since 2003. She is married to Barry MacIntosh and they reside in Lake Orion, Michigan.

**Peter LaBarbera** is Founder and President of Americans For Truth About Homosexuality (AFTAH), an organization based outside Chicago that exposes and counters the LGBTQ (lesbian, gay, bisexual, transgender, queer) movement. He is also a writer for LifeSiteNews.com. A former reporter for the *Washington Times*, Peter served as executive director of the Illinois Family Institute, and as a writer, editor and analyst for both the Family Research Council and Concerned Women for America. He has done thousands of radio, TV and print media interviews, most dealing with LGBTQ and morality issues. Peter has been happily married to his wife Cristina for 29 years. They are the blessed parents of five children.

**Dr. Tina Trent** writes about crime, political radicals, social movements, and academia. She has worked as a conservative political organizer and lobbyist in Florida and Georgia and blogs about crime and politics at www.tinatrent.com. She published several in-depth reports for America's Survival and its Soros Files project. Tina also helped the late Larry Grathwohl release a new edition of Larry's 1976 memoir, *Bringing Down America: An FBI Informer with the Weathermen*, an account of his time infiltrating the Weather Underground. Dr. Trent attended New College in Sarasota, where she first encountered some of the key leaders of the psychedelic legalization movement described in this report. She holds a doctorate from the Institute for Women's Studies of Emory University, where, under the tutelage of conservative, pro-life scholar Elizabeth Fox-Genovese, she wrote about the negative effect of social movements and popular culture on criminal law. Dr. Trent also spent more than a decade in Atlanta's worst neighborhoods, providing social services to refugees, troubled families, and crime victims, and discovering first-hand the destruction caused by leftist politics and the poverty industry, an experience she describes as "the reason I'm now a practicing Catholic, a registered Republican, and a social conservative."

# Table of Contents

# The Age of Moral Suicide

By Cliff Kincaid

Conservatives who think Barack Hussein Obama's legacy has been dismantled by President Donald J. Trump are fooling themselves. Obama's legacy continues through the Deep State, and his influence is still a powerful force in the judicial branch.

Andrew Sullivan, described as one of the top political and cultural pundits of our time, has said that,[1] in his opinion, there were only "a couple of shifts" under the Obama presidency "that do indeed seem to be as permanent as anything is in politics." He named these as "marriage equality and legal cannabis."

In regard to marijuana and other drugs, we are entering the *Brave New World* of Aldous Huxley, where Soma is prescribed for the population, to keep them distracted or content, or, in this case, to spark the "expansion of consciousness." This book tells the story in shocking detail.

So-called "marriage equality" was imposed by the Supreme Court in what the late Justice Antonin Scalia called a judicial "Putsch," a sudden attempt to overthrow our form of government. The "marriage equality" ruling, authored by Justice Anthony Kennedy, subverted states' rights by overturning state laws and constitutional provisions nationwide regarding the definition of marriage. Like Roe v. Wade, which legalized abortion on demand, it was an example of a judicial ruling not based on law or the Constitution.

While President Trump has been trying to remake courts dominated by Obama appointees and other liberals, what has been lacking is an effort by the Trump Administration and Congress to remove or restrict the power of tyrannical judges who present their own liberal personal opinions as expressions of the facts and the law.

In her book, *The Supremacists: The Tyranny of Judges and How to Stop It,* the late conservative leader Phyllis Schlafly wrote, "The cancer of judicial supremacy will not go away until the American people rise up and repudiate it. It's time for the American people to notify their elected representatives, federal and state, that it is their mission to restore the Constitution with its proper balance among the three branches of the federal government. We must save self-government from the rule of judges. The whole future of America depends on it."

In regard to the judicial success of the homosexual rights movement, journalist Peter LaBarbera examines whether Obama's alleged personal involvement in homosexuality was a factor in his embrace of the movement as president. Obama biographer David Maraniss admits that Obama wrote a poem about his mentor, communist Frank Marshall Davis, called "Pop," with some strange lines about stains and smells on shorts. "He looks at Pop and sees something that repels him and attracts him, that he wants to run away from yet knows he must embrace," Maraniss wrote, as if to explain what Obama was thinking and doing. Writer Jack Cashill had also suggested that "Pop" was Davis and that the poem had definite "sexual overtones." We are left wondering what Davis, a pedophile and dope smoker, did to a young Obama.[2]

Such a relationship may explain  Obama policies as president to use the full force of government to allow men and boys to enter girls' restrooms and locker rooms, even in the K-12 public schools. [3] It was a policy of presidential perversion.

Obama also approved acceptance of transgenders and sex change operations in the U.S. Armed Forces.

Like Davis, who wrote *Sex Rebel: Black*, Obama was a sex rebel. As writer Andrew Walden has noted, the term "Sex Rebel" was meant to characterize Davis's rebellion against American society, another part of the communist revolution, which was a way to strike back against religion and its strictures on promiscuous sexual activity. Perversion was a central aspect of Davis's communist identity. It was a major part of Obama's presidency and legacy.

Many people do not know that the Communist Manifesto called for the abolition of the traditional family, in addition to the abolition of private property. "Families and the moral order stand firmly in the way of any socialist revolution," notes conservative writer Robert Knight.

Treason

One of the most bizarre spectacles in the course of our nation's history was the case of Army intelligence analyst Bradley Manning, a homosexual who became "transgendered" in prison, with the help of hormone treatments paid for by U.S. taxpayers, and became a "she" by the name of Chelsea. Incredibly, the Defense Department hosted a Lesbian, Gay, Bisexual and Transgender Pride Month event as Manning was on trial for espionage and treason. Obama later freed Manning from prison after only serving 7 years of a 35-year sentence. [4]

Senator Tom Cotton (R-Ark.) said, "When I was leading soldiers in Afghanistan, Private Manning was undermining us by leaking hundreds of thousands of classified documents to WikiLeaks. I don't understand why the president [Obama] would feel special compassion for someone who endangered the lives of our troops, diplomats, intelligence officers, and allies. We ought not treat a traitor like a martyr."

Manning then ran for the Senate in Maryland on the Democratic Party ticket. His political platform included:

- Open borders.
- Universal healthcare.
- Universal basic income.

- Ending the "police state."
- Eliminating the "military industrial complex."
- Defending unions, and
- Ending "mass surveillance."

Reports also surfaced that Manning had posted a picture of himself/herself on a ledge preparing to jump to his/her death.

The "fundamental transformation" of America under Obama could also be seen in the spectacle of the Satanic-looking drag queen, Xochi Mochi, reading to little children for Drag Queen Story Hour at the Michelle Obama Public Library in Long Beach, California. Mochi read Todd Parr's children's book *It's Okay to be Different* to the children on October 14, 2017.

George W. Draper's important book, *Diversity and Inclusion: What You Don't Know and Why You Don't Know It,* notes that Obama's Executive Order 13583, "Establishing a Coordinated Government-wide Initiative to Promote Diversity and Inclusion in the Federal Workforce," has encouraged the enemies within. On October 5, 2016, Obama issued a follow-up presidential memorandum "Promoting Diversity and Inclusion in the National Security Workforce," specifically targeting the Intelligence Community. These executive orders reduce employment standards, waive job qualifications, ignore the dangers of incompatible cultural behaviors and ideas, and reject American moral standards.

Hence, we have people in the Intelligence Community who have no allegiance to America or its traditional values. At the time Manning was stealing documents for WikiLeaks, he was an active participant in the homosexual subculture, under the noses of his military superiors, and even went to gay bars. He had advertised his homosexuality on Facebook.

The powerful forces in the Deep State pushing these policies of treason and subversion are why Dr. Mark Green, a West Point grad and decorated U.S. Army flight surgeon, was forced out of consideration for the job as Secretary of the Army. Trump had nominated him but accepted his withdrawal just four weeks after the "false and misleading attacks" had started against him. One of Green's so-called objectionable comments was the science-based and common-sense belief, made in his capacity as a Tennessee state senator, that most psychiatrists believe transgenderism is "a disease." He referred to the Diagnostic and Statistical Manual of Mental Disorders as having listed transgenderism as a disorder to be treated. The National Center for Transgender Equality, funded by leftist billionaire George Soros, had denounced Green as "hateful" for standing up for biology and science.

In total, the Open Society Foundations of George Soros have already funneled $14 billion into a progressive infrastructure that includes literally dozens of groups designed to marginalize conservatives and promote left-wing causes such as drug legalization, the rights of "sex workers" and felons, euthanasia, radical feminism, abortion rights, and homosexual and transgender rights. Soros subsequently transferred an additional $18 billion to his foundation to carry on this work in the future. He told the *Washington Post* on June 10, 2018, that he would "push even harder" in the age of Trump "for his agenda."

Marijuana, Mental Illness, and Violence

Andrew Sullivan's reference to the other shift, on marijuana policy, is significant. In an article titled, "Yes, I'm Dependent on Weed," he admitted being a "daily stoner" and acknowledged the drug's harmful effects.[5] While it is legal in some states and legalization has certainly created a politically significant group of stoners in society, marijuana is still not legal under federal law.

The *Journal of Addiction Research & Therapy* has published a ground-breaking analysis of how marijuana is linked to violence, mental illness and even jihad. [6] Marijuana, the authors of the report say, can spark psychosis and paranoia, and thus contribute to terroristic thoughts and exacerbate aggressive behavior. It noted the case of the Tsarnaev brothers, who killed three and injured 264 others with bombs at the Boston Marathon on April 5, 2013. They were born in the former Soviet Union and attended a mosque in the Boston area and were known as heavy marijuana users. Other cases involving marijuana and violence include Eddie Routh, the vet thought to have

PTSD who killed both Chris Kyle ("American Sniper") and Chad Littlefield. He was diagnosed with cannabis-induced psychosis.

Free trade policies provide perfect cover for drug trafficking and drug-money laundering. The North American Free Trade Agreement (NAFTA) -- a pact to spur business activity by lowering trade barriers and reducing border inspections between the United States, Canada, and Mexico -- facilitated drug trafficking into the United States from Mexico.

The Communist role in international drug trafficking was documented in the book *Red Cocaine* by Joseph Douglass, Jr. The purpose of the Communist campaign was not only to demoralize the West but raise hard currency and identify drug users who could be blackmailed for intelligence purposes.

Under a U.N.-sponsored plan to legalize drugs on a worldwide basis, as recommended by the George Soros-funded Global Commission on Drug Policy, drug trafficking countries such as Mexico would become "respectable." Notorious drug traffickers and their bankers would be transformed into legitimate businessmen. As Dr. Tina Trent documents in her chapter of this book, this plan has been unfolding in the U.S. under Obama. President Trump can and should stop it.

According to drug policy expert David G. Evans, the currently available high potency marijuana not only can cause mental illness but is responsible for birth defects, low birth weights for babies, more emergency room visits, an increasing number of school problems, and violence. Cases of "scromiting," or screaming while vomiting, have been linked to marijuana use.

It turns out that Soros, the main funder of the drug legalization movement, is in business with Trump son-in-law Jared Kushner, who is very liberal on marijuana and "prison reform."[7] Together with libertarian billionaire Peter Thiel and Senator Cory Gardner, these forces want to pass a bill to protect the marijuana industry from federal anti-drug laws. (Thiel supported Ron Paul for president in 2012).

But the states don't have the resources to cope with the damage. Under the cover of legalization, Mexican cartels are moving into states like Colorado and California and not only destroying lives but the environment with illegal pesticides and fungicides that are seeping into the groundwater that children drink. [8] "The states are dominated by the marijuana industry," Evans says.

From Marijuana to LSD

In her chapter of this book, Trent describes how the Obama Administration facilitated the use of marijuana and how, building off the successes of the Soros-funded marijuana movement, a group called the Multidisciplinary Association for Psychedelic Studies (MAPS) is now demanding acceptance of "psychedelics," or mind-altering drugs that create hallucinations. Although marijuana itself is a hallucinogen, MAPS is proposing easy access to "psychedelic medicine," including LSD and Ecstasy.

Trent notes that drugs are seen as another means by which Christianity can be neutralized.

MAPS President Rick Doblin once described himself to *High Times* magazine as an "LSD therapist," after "having taken LSD rather often." He took LSD guru Timothy Leary's advice to "turn on, tune in, drop out," before going back to college and eventually starting MAPS in 1986. "His undergraduate thesis at New College of Florida was a 25-year follow-up to the classic Good Friday Experiment, which evaluated the potential of psychedelic drugs to catalyze religious experiences," his bio says. He then completed a Ph.D. at Harvard's John F. Kennedy School of Government. Indeed, according to a story about the "Good Friday Experiment," which occurred in 1962, participants took hallucinogenic drugs and then attended a Good Friday worship service. They were later evaluated as to whether the drugs could produce "pseudo-mystical states."

Obama's Drug History

As he was growing up under the direction of Frank Marshall Davis, the communist who functioned as his father figure, a young Obama became a member of the "Choom Gang," a group of heavy marijuana users who understood ways to make the "high" from the drug even more powerful and lasting. One method they used was to smoke dope in a car and then inhale what was left of the smoke in the ceiling of the car.

As president, Obama did little to stop the heroin epidemic that disproportionately affects white communities devastated by bad trade deals and open borders. Several researchers have used the phrase "Deaths of despair" to refer to what is happening in the "heroin beltway" of America. The opioid crisis stems, in part, from a law passed by Congress and signed by Obama that allowed drug companies to increase distribution of these drugs. Mexican heroin continues to come across the border and Chinese labs are producing and exporting deadly synthetic drugs, like fentanyl. Tens of thousands of Americans are being killed every year.

Heroin injection centers are being planned for liberal cities, to enable addicts to get high at taxpayer expense.

The HSBC bank allowed Mexican drug cartels and terrorist groups to launder dirty money through the U.S. financial system but the Obama Administration did not prosecute bank officials on criminal charges. The House Financial Services Committee released a staff report of its investigation into the U.S. Department of Justice's decision not to prosecute HSBC. One of the findings was that:

> Senior DOJ leadership, including Attorney General [Eric] Holder, overruled an internal recommendation by DOJ's Asset Forfeiture and Money Laundering Section to prosecute HSBC because of DOJ leadership's concern

that prosecuting the bank would have serious adverse consequences on the financial system.[9]

The Obama Administration was also accused of obstructing justice in probes regarding alleged drug-trafficking and money-laundering schemes tied to the Hezbollah terror group. [10] In the scheme known as Fast and Furious, the administration authorized a gun-running operation that put deadly weapons in the hands of narcotics traffickers from Mexico.

Oprah and the Stoners

In her chapter, "From Oprah to Obama and Beyond," Constance Cumbey notes that Oprah Winfrey has gone beyond promoting kooky New Age ideas to recommending drugs for her mostly female readers. The April 2018 edition of her "Oprah Magazine" featured the article, "Is Marijuana the New Merlot?" Another article, "Mom's Guide to Not Getting Busted," advised women how to use dope "without getting into trouble."

Nevertheless, Oprah is an icon. "Watching Oprah," an exhibition at the Smithsonian's National Museum of African American History and Culture, recently opened, presenting the billionaire as a role model (Oprah gave the museum $21 million). It notes she has received eight awards from GLAAD for "LGBTQ acceptance" and positive portrayals of lesbian, gay, bisexual, transgender and queer people.

"The Oprah Winfrey Show remains the highest-rated daytime talk show in American television history," the exhibit says. Obama used Oprah's influence in his successful run for president in 2008. Interestingly, Oprah recently signed a multi-year deal with Apple for a new streaming service that will compete with Netflix, another streaming service that made a deal with Barack Obama.

Who Was Barack Hussein Obama?

These cultural "shifts," as Andrew Sullivan describes them, are profound. They reflect the character of America's first black president with a Muslim background, Barack Hussein Obama, once known as Barry Soetoro, and his billionaire backers.

On one level, the "shifts" reflect the "permanent revolution" of constant change and struggle articulated by Karl Marx, the father of communism. On another level, they reflect the power of what is called the Deep State and its commitment to the revolutionary upheaval in moral standards that is destroying America. The Deep State is an entity of current and former officials who protect themselves at the expense of the public's right to know about their corrupt practices.

The bureaucratic and administrative power that characterizes the Deep State, no matter who wins the presidency, can be seen in then-acting FBI Director Andrew McCabe bringing the LGBTQ lobby, with "Q" meaning queer, into the FBI itself – at a time when Trump was already president. McCabe hosted the June 15, 2017, annual "Intelligence Community (IC) Pride." The featured speaker was Nicole Cozier, the Director of Diversity and Inclusion at the Human Rights Campaign, who had previously worked for Planned Parenthood. The Human Rights Campaign endorsed Obama for election and re-election.

So-called breakout sessions were held to discuss such matters as "Deconstructing the Binary and Ditching the Identity Hierarchy."

The $60 billion a year intelligence community is hiring what the government itself used to call "sexual perverts" but is now calling "Secret Agents of Change." A conference entitled, "America's LGBT Spies: Secret Agents (of Change)," was actually held in collaboration with the U.S. Intelligence Community.

But these secret agents are not identifying or fighting the enemy. They are subverting our government from within, bringing down America's traditional values and moral strength in the process. Their hero was Barack Hussein Obama.

Indeed, Obama's Director of National Intelligence James Clapper and FBI Director James Comey were listed as speakers at the "Fifth Annual Intelligence Community Pride Summit" to salute "America's LGBT Spies." [11] It is never explained how mentally ill people unsure of their own sexual identities can help safeguard our nation. On the contrary, they are an illustration of our decadence as a nation and inability to understand what national survival is all about.

How the KGB Exploits Perversion

John Barron, in his book, *KGB: The Secret Work of Soviet Secret Agents*, said that, "Contrary to popular supposition, the [Soviet] KGB is not primarily interested in homosexuals because of their presumed susceptibility to blackmail." Instead, he said:

> In its judgment, homosexuality often is accompanied by personality disorders that make the victim potentially unstable and vulnerable to adroit manipulation. It hunts the particular homosexual who, while more or less a functioning member of his society, is nevertheless subconsciously at war with it and himself.
>
> Compulsively driven into tortured relations that never gratify, he cannot escape awareness that he is different. Being different, he easily rationalizes that he is not morally bound by the mores, values, and allegiances that unite others in community and society. Moreover, he nurtures a dormant impulse to strike back at the society which he feels has conspired to make him a secret leper. To such a man, treason offers the weapon of retaliation.

Barron's description seems to describe almost perfectly the case of Bradley/Chelsea Manning.

To its credit, the Trump Administration did rescind the Obama-era letter designed to allow boys into girls' bathrooms [12] and Trump has tried to implement a transgender ban and reverse Obama's policy of paying for transgender surgeries in the military. While the Pentagon did not officially celebrate LGBT Pride month in June of 2018, a Department of Defense LGBT group held an event, along with a Pride Happy Hour at a local bar.

What's more, the *Washington Blade* reported:

> The State Department has continued to support LGBT and intersex rights abroad since President Trump took office... The State Department this year [2017] acknowledged Pride month, the Transgender Day of Remembrance and Intersex Awareness Day.

Former Fox News personality Heather Nauert, now the Acting Under Secretary for Public Diplomacy and Public Affairs and State Department Spokesperson, said on March 26, 2018:

> I am proud to work for an Administration that has been vocal in its support for protecting LGBTI persons from violence and discrimination. Whether for Pride Month, Spirit Day, National Coming Out Day, Intersex Awareness Day, or Transgender Day of Remembrance, we have spoken out in strong support of the liberty, dignity, and the

human rights of LGBTI persons worldwide. We will continue to do so. [13]

Honorees at the 2017 Trans Equality Awards, co-sponsored by the CIA, included Vanita Gupta, the former Obama Justice Department official who led the effort to force transgender bathrooms and locker rooms on schools as a condition of funding. When the 2018 Trans Equality Now Awards was held on May 17, 2018, at The Hamilton in Washington D.C., it is no surprise that Obama adviser Valerie Jarrett was given an award for being an "ally" of the transgender movement.

In fact, the Soros-funded National Center for Transgender Equality (NCTE) has held two conferences in a row, 2017 and 2018, whose sponsors have included the CIA. Other sponsors of the 2018 conference, which paid tribute to the Obama Administration for its transgender policies, included Amazon, Facebook, Google, and the Big Pharma giant Gilead.

Walt Heyer, a former transgender, says, "The CIA is suborning the erosion of the church and biblical foundation of marriage. This erosion of the biblical foundation of the family will ultimately replace all moral boundaries leading to social chaos."

Under Obama, the government worked with the homosexual lobby to isolate and cut off aid to countries like Uganda for opposing homosexuality. Ugandan Christian minister Martin

Ssempa had issued a strong rebuttal to Obama's criticism of his country for considering passage of a law to discourage and punish certain homosexual practices. "Sodomy is neither the change we want nor can believe in," he said. Ssempa tells me he is working on a book that includes a chapter on how Obama's legacy "needs to be dismantled for our families and faith to survive."

Communist Infiltration

The CIA website still features a statement from Obama CIA director John Brennan on the role played by the CIA's "Executive Diversity and Inclusion Council" and the "Center for Mission Diversity and Inclusion." Brennan's "CIA Diversity and Inclusion Strategy" recognizes the need to hire "Lesbian, Gay, Bisexual, and Transgender Individuals."

Brennan himself voted for the Communist Party when he was in college, before he joined the CIA. Apparently, hiring communists has become another element of federal "diversity" policies. Questions persist about whether Brennan, an alumnus of Catholic Fordham University, converted to Islam and why he took his oath of office on a copy of the U.S. Constitution and not the Bible.

It appears communists are also allowed to join the U.S. military. A West Point cadet, Spenser Rapone, was photographed wearing a Che Guevara T-shirt under his uniform and wrote "communism will win" under his cap. After the photograph came to light, an investigation was launched, he ultimately resigned his commission, and was reportedly separated from the Army with an Other Than Honorable discharge. He was then scheduled for a Socialism 2018 conference in Chicago. However, the official U.S. Army response to queries on Rapone consisted of:

> Due to privacy act restrictions, we are limited in what information we can provide. We can confirm, however, that the Army conducted a full investigation, and that appropriate action was taken. We now consider the matter closed.

Retired Lt. Col. Robert M. Heffington, who had quit teaching at West Point, revealed:

> ...standards at West Point are nonexistent. They exist on paper, but nowhere else. The senior administration at West Point inexplicably refuses to enforce West Point's publicly touted high standards on cadets, and, having picked up on this, cadets refuse to enforce standards on each other. The Superintendent refuses to enforce admissions standards or the cadet Honor Code, the Dean refuses to enforce academic standards, and the Commandant refuses to enforce standards of conduct and discipline. [14]

Rapone had outed himself. The question remains whether there are other communists in the military keeping mum about their ideological hatred of the United States.

As for the CIA, it defends hiring transgenders and sponsoring transgender conferences. When I asked the CIA about its sponsorship of the Trans Equality Awards, a spokesman responded:

> CIA is participating in the 2018 Trans Equality Now Awards event to let people in the transgender community know about scholarship, internship, and career opportunities at CIA. CIA regards our country's diversity as an asset that we can leverage to gain strategic advantage over our adversaries.

One of the CIA's employee groups is the Agency Network of Gay, Lesbian, Bisexual, and Transgender Officers and Allies.

What the intelligence agencies are doing, through their hiring of LGBTQ individuals, is embracing the very same movement of moral decadence that began in Soviet Russia and destroyed the moral fiber of the Russian people through sexual perversion and abortion. Today, Russia is fast becoming a Muslim nation because native Russians are dying out and not reproducing. "Strategically Russia is surrendering to the Muslim world," notes former KGB officer Konstantin Preobrazhensky. "The Russian population is declining rapidly," having been undermined by the "communist experiment." Now America is going through that "experiment."

The shocking facts have been provided by radical activist Bini Adamczak, the author of a fascinating book that carries the title, *Communism for Kids.* She has written that, "With the [Russian] revolution, the right to legal abortion, both sexes' right to divorce, the decriminalization of adultery, and the annulment of the sodomy law (which had previously prohibited homosexuality) were implemented and enforced." In Moscow, one could find international communes led by "gay communists," she says. "Drag kings could become legitimate members of the Red Army. Participants of the revolutionary debates decided upon the destruction of the family, demanded the legalization of incest, and advertised the practice [of] polygamy." [15] One writer confirms, "There was a certain tolerance and even gay liberation in the early years of the Soviet Union, before homosexuality was re-criminalized in 1933 and the community went back underground." [16]

While "Queer Communism" was then suppressed in the Soviet Union, it has thrived in the West.

Just as the modern-day homosexual rights movement in America was founded by a communist (who also believed in the occult) by the name of Harry Hay, the movement to make men into women was initially funded and set in motion by a suspected communist, Reed Erickson. He had campaigned for Henry Wallace for president in 1948 on the ticket of the communist-dominated Progressive Party. Wallace was, for a time, involved in Theosophy, which teaches that man can become God through mystical experiences, and can even perform miracles.

Erickson's foundation, financed with tens of millions of dollars from his family fortune, focused on homosexuality and what was called "transsexualism." Later, its emphasis was "new age spirituality." [17] He fled America after being charged with using illegal drugs and died in Mexico at his "Love Joy Palace" from his addiction to those drugs. Clearly, despite his ability to buy acceptance as a transgender, he could not live with the changes that he had forced on himself. It is a reminder that gender identity problems should be treated with psychological and psychiatric counseling, not chemicals and surgeries.

Yet his influence has been recognized by the LGBT Funders group in its 2015 "Transformational Impact" report. Referring to the work of the Reed Erickson Foundation, the report paid tribute to him/her, noting "the main focuses of the foundation's work were gay rights, transgender communities, and New Age spirituality."

Another key figure was Shawn Hailey, also known as Ashawna, who supported Obama's campaign for president and was a member of the board of directors of the Multidisciplinary Association for Psychedelic Studies. Shawn Hailey was born a man, but changed his gender to female and his name to Ashawna. She passed away in 2011 and left $5.5 million to the organization. She made her money through high-tech companies in Silicon Valley and was a co-founder of Meta Software Corporation, which was sold to Avanti Corporation in 1996. She was also a strong supporter of the Marijuana Policy Project, the Soros-backed Drug Policy Alliance, Code Pink and the American Civil Liberties Union.  In total, she left over $10 million to the liberal-left.

The sexual perversion and the drugs reflect the collapse of moral standards. An Obama CIA director, General David Petraeus, committed adultery and was caught. He admitted lying to FBI agents about the affair but didn't serve any prison time.  In the FBI, two employees involved in the Hillary Clinton and Donald J. Trump investigations, Peter Strzok and Lisa Page, were having an extramarital affair that was known within the bureau. The *Washington Post* actually reported that "Defenders of Strzok and Page inside the FBI said that because there was no direct supervisory role between Page and Strzok in the workplace, there wasn't anything professionally wrong about having an affair…" The paper went on to say, however, that if a foreign intelligence agency learned of such an affair, "they could try to use it as a means of blackmail…" It was then reported that a *New York Times* reporter covering Russia-gate was dating the "security director" of the Senate Intelligence Committee.

The evidence we released at our November 10, 2017, National Press Club conference on Russia-gate demonstrates that the investigation of President

Trump, unleashed by Obama and his operatives as he was leaving the White House, was a disinformation operation using our own intelligence agencies that came to rely in part on Russian sources in the so-called Trump Dossier. It was a clever maneuver on the part of Obama, Hillary, and their Russian backers. The Russians did not want their influence operations in the Obama Administration exposed. You may recall that Anna Chapman, a sexy Russian spy, was accused of seducing an unnamed cabinet official in the Obama administration in an effort to obtain classified information. She was one of several Russian agents caught and quickly expelled from the U.S. in 2010. She returned to Russia and was honored with an award at a Kremlin ceremony.

To understand how a nation falls into the hands of its enemies and adversaries, the book, *The Rise of Gay Rights and the Fall of the British Empire: Liberal Resistance and the Bloomsbury Group,* is highly recommended. It examines how an elite and influential group of perverts can affect and infect a nation.

As the title implies, the author, David A.J. Richards, the Edwin D. Webb Professor of Law at New York University School of Law, asserts that the rise of what was at first a secret homosexual movement in Britain corresponds with the decline of the nation as a world power. He argues that the homosexual movement is a form of "resistance" to the foundations of Western civilization and "imperialism." Of course, he welcomes the decline of Western power and tradition.

Britain's Moral Collapse

The so-called "Cambridge Five," the most damaging spies in British history who all secretly worked for the Soviet KGB, were members of this elite group. Stephen Koch, in his excellent book, *Double Lives. Spies and Writers in the Secret War of Ideas Against the West*, writes that the fact that so many of the Cambridge spies were homosexual can be "traced" to the influence of Lytton Strachey and the Bloomsbury group. Koch writes:

> My suspicion is that Anthony Blunt and Guy Burgess [two of the Cambridge Five] used their own shrewdness to make their Soviet controls see how a homosexual coterie based on Strachey's model [the Bloomsbury group] could be exploited, both in its unstated loyalties and its unstated possibilities for blackmail, and thereby form the basis for an espionage ring.[18]

Strachey was a homosexual, socialist and sadomasochist who engaged in a mock crucifixion and "believed his attitude to sex was 100 years ahead of its time." [19]

In Britain today, except for some talk about making bureaucracy more efficient, the British Conservative Party has become a laughingstock in terms of promoting limited government and traditional moral values. What's more, it has moved far to the left in order to attract votes from the sexually different. Christian preachers there are being arrested for speaking out against homosexuality. British activist Tommy Robinson was locked up for his public opposition to jihad and attempt to expose sexual abuse among its Muslim followers.

Targeting Children

In America, we see how a similar group of elites facilitate this ongoing "transformation" of America, to use Obama's phrase, and have no compunction about destroying the morals of young people.

The leadership of the Boy Scouts of America (BSA), which once advised young men to be "morally straight," was pressured to admit open homosexuals [20] and then to drop the word "boy" from the name. Boys are now running in girls' track and field events in high schools. On the professional level, most Major League Baseball teams host LGBT "pride nights," with the St. Louis Cardinals asking transgendered activist "Tassandra Crush" to throw out the first pitch at a game in 2017. The National Football League has launched an LGBTQ employee affinity group, NFL Pride.

Pope Francis, one of the most liberal popes in history, seems to draw the line at transgenderism, telling the 23rd General Assembly of the Members of the Pontifical Academy for Life that the process of "radically neutralizing sexual difference" contradicts the divine plan for humanity. He said, "The biological and psychical manipulation of sexual difference, which biomedical technology allows us to perceive as completely available to free choice – which it is not! – thus risks dismantling the source of energy that nurtures the alliance between man and woman and which renders it creative and fruitful." [21]

However, Francis seems to be comfortable with someone identifying as inherently homosexual. The Church, of course, has been badly compromised by homosexuals in its ranks who sexually abused children. (The Catechism of the Catholic Church continues to describe homosexuality as "grave depravity," and the homosexual inclination as "intrinsically disordered.")

Pope Francis lectures the world on global warming and capitalism but can't clean up the corruption in his own church. Randy Engel discussed her book, *The Rite of Sodomy: Homosexuality and the Roman Catholic Church*, during an appearance on ASI TV. She names the names. She takes the inquiry way beyond the results of the Oscar-winning film "Spotlight," based on the *Boston Globe* investigations of pedophile priests and cover-ups in Boston.

Indeed, an entire chapter of Engel's book examines the Cambridge spies and what she calls the Homintern -- a homosexual network in England, Europe and the United States that was exploited by the Soviet Union and other Communist powers during the Cold War. She links this to the Communist infiltration of the Church, and its possible connection to the rise of a homosexual clergy.

Appearing on ASI TV, Mary McAlister of Liberty Counsel says we are witnessing "the satanic sexualization of our children and the destruction of the family."

Obama Education Department official Kevin Jennings was among those who were "inspired" to lead a life of homosexual activism by Harry Hay, the founder of the modern homosexual rights movement in the U.S. A prominent member of the Communist Party USA, Hay was a supporter of the North American Man-Boy Love Association (NAMBLA) and self-proclaimed "Radical Faerie" who wore dresses and believed in the power of the occult. Transgender liberation is the next major frontier.

*Communism for Kids* author Bini Adamczak says that even more advances have to be made in the field of "queer politics," using the strategies of Marxist revolution. Eventually, "modern reproduction technologies" could be used to "completely abolish the sexes."

She notes that the last words of Leslie Feinberg, a Marxist member of the Workers World Party and a transgender, were, "Remember me as a revolutionary communist. Hasten the revolution!"

Academia is helping to hasten the revolution. The University of Maryland hosted a "Queer Beyond Repair" conference that included a keynote speech on the future of the sexual device known as the dildo. Titles of other topics or panels at the University of Maryland event included:

- How a Girl Becomes a Ship.
- Black Queerness and Trans Bodies.
- Traveling to Dark Places: Race, Touch, and Sadomasochism.

An April 14, 2018, "TRANS(Form)Ing Queer" event at the University of Maryland featured such topics as "psychedelic sexology." [22]

Madness and Suicide

Former transgender Walt Heyer calls this "madness," noting that nobody can prove transgenders exist, and that the scientific evidence demonstrates there is "too much unhappiness and too many suicides" from the chemical and surgical procedure to justify the process of changing one's biological sex. Individuals in this condition are suffering from deeper psychological issues, Heyer observes, adding, "Psychologically and emotionally healthy people do not attempt suicide but trans-folks do." He called the transgender movement "the greatest medical and social fraud of the last 50 years." [23]

Yet the intelligence community not only condones but celebrates it. Hence, we can expect recruiting of LGBT spies from within communist organizations.

Trump's first CIA director, Mike Pompeo, had said that WikiLeaks, whose founder Julian Assange worked for Russian TV, "walks like a hostile intelligence service and talks like a hostile intelligence service. It has encouraged its followers to find jobs at CIA in order to obtain intelligence. It directed Chelsea Manning in her theft of specific secret information. And it overwhelmingly focuses on the United States, while seeking support from anti-democratic countries and organizations."

But Pompeo did not disclose whether he had investigated the lax rules that are in place at the CIA and other intelligence agencies, permitting mentally disordered and confused transgender individuals to gain employment and get top secret security clearances.

By their own estimates, 41 percent of transgenders attempt suicide (compared to 1.5 percent of the general population) and transgender women are 49 times more likely to acquire HIV (the virus that causes AIDS) than the general population. [24] These figures come from the group, Funders for LGBTQ Issues, which cites the Soros-funded Open Society Foundations as the number one funder of domestic and global trans issues for the period 2011-2013.

The emergence of Soros as the major funder of the left has enabled the Russians to abandon communism in a dialectical manuever that makes them appear nationalistic, religious, and even "conservative" on the world stage. Soros underwrites the global left while Putin appeals to the conservatives in the West as a Christian statesman.[25] There is absolutely no evidence, aside from rhetoric, to suggest that Russia in general and Russian President Vladimir Putin in particular have been converted to Christianity.

Instead, what we are witnessing is a massive Russian "active measures" campaign that has ensnared many American conservatives, convincing them that Putin is somehow a legitimate alternative to the globalism of Obama and the European Union. [26]

But Soros is not alone in financing the forces of Cultural Marxism in the West. Writer Jennifer Bilek has documented "the money flowing from the elites" such as Soros into the movement to put men in women's restrooms and identifies them as also including Jennifer Pritzker (a male who identifies as transgender); Martine Rothblatt (a male who identifies as transgender and transhumanist); Tim Gill (a gay man); Drummond Pike; Warren Buffett's family; Jon Stryker (a gay man); Mark Bonham (a gay man); and Ric Weiland (a deceased gay man whose philanthropy is still LGBT-oriented). "Most of these billionaires fund the transgender lobby and organizations through their own organizations, including corporations," she writes, contending that they "are not only influencing, but actually dictating to governments the institutionalization and normalization of gender identity ideology." [27] This is the real Deep State.

The Buffett connection is very significant. Billionaire Warren Buffett has been depicted as a great humanitarian and philanthropist when he has poured tens of millions of dollars into the morally objectionable cause of promoting abortion not only here but throughout the developing world. He is also a big supporter of the U.N.

Warren Buffett is Peter Buffett's father and has donated many millions to his NoVo Foundation. Peter Buffett is co-chair of NoVo Foundation, which in collaboration with Jon Stryker of ARCUS poured millions into the trans lobby in 2015. Specifically, the Arcus Foundation and the NoVo Foundation announced a Global Trans Initiative that will donate at least $20 million over five years to transgender-focused organizations and activists. [28]

Bilek notes that Jennifer Pritzker is a cousin to Penny Pritzker, who served on President Obama's Council for Jobs and Competitiveness, Economic Recovery Advisory Board, and as Commerce Secretary. Penny was national co-chair of Obama for America 2012 and national finance chair of Obama's 2008 presidential campaign. "To say she was influential in getting President Obama elected would be an understatement," she adds. Bilek also noted that Soros and Gill were two of the major transgender movement funders who generated millions of dollars to get Obama elected, and Stryker was one of the top five contributors to Obama's campaign. Warren Buffett is closely tied with the Pritzker family financially. [29]

In addition to these personalities playing a role in getting Obama to facilitate the transgender movement, Bilek notes "there has been an explosion in transgender medical infrastructure across the United States," with gender clinics, pharmaceutical companies, hospitals, and other medical institutions "clamoring to get on board with the new developments."

Funders of the World Professional Association for Transgender Health (WPATH), formerly known as the Harry Benjamin International Gender Dysphoria Association, include more than a dozen members of the medical industrial complex profiting from pushing hormonal treatments and surgeries on people. It has become a big business.

Obama was the first president to mention transgenders in a State of the Union address. By doing so, he made them into another special interest group, to be cultivated for political purposes. This is how a Marxist political movement grows – by identifying more alleged victims of oppression and the capitalist structure. Obama knows the process well, having learned the tactics of political organizing in Chicago from organizers trained by Saul Alinsky (with the support of the Catholic Church). This is the Marxist "permanent revolution."

Everybody is Trans

The implications go far beyond the small percentage of people who want to engage in genital mutilation to change sexes. Stella Morabito, a well-known writer on these topics, tells me, "Here's the crux of it all: the transgender ideology insists that EVERYBODY is trans. They won't confess to it just yet, but it's embedded in their 'sex assigned at birth' meme -- a premise that is planted in all transgender law and which is designed to apply universally. (It de-sexes everybody in law.) Their advocates need to be pinned down on why they are imposing their ideology on everybody. The administrative state is, of course, a

40

part of the swamp and has co-opted the corporate world into transgenderism -- as well as into many other such vehicles being used primarily to consolidate power."

"If we construct our own gods, we will also construct our own sexual identities," writes Dr. Peter Jones, one of the world's foremost experts on paganism and the occult.

This phase of Marxist revolution can also be considered a major element of the New Age Movement. Constance Cumbey outlines in this book how a growing group of people in America and the world have broken with the Judeo-Christian tradition to instead endorse the notion of God as a mystical force inhabiting humans, the earth, or spiritual "masters." These people sometimes practice "transcendental meditation," a form of "communication" with spiritual forces that has also been adopted and promoted by the Vatican at an April 26-28, 2018 conference. Emmy-award winning Dr. Mehmet Oz, also known as "Dr. Oz, who rose to fame on "The Oprah Winfrey Show," was featured among the broadcast moderators at the event. He is a Muslim with a passion for Islamic mysticism. [30]

What is the New Age Movement?

In order to understand the New Age Movement and how it radically differs from Christianity, some basic facts about the philosophy of religion need to be addressed. There are three general theologies about the ultimate status of man and God:

- Man is distant from and radically different than God.
- Man is identical to and at one with God, and
- Man is distant from and radically different than God but that man becomes one with God through mediation, the Christ or Messiah.

The New Age Movement incorporates the second option, which is attained through awareness, meditation, altered states of consciousness, or evolution into the oneness. But it also incorporates part of the third option, as the followers of the New Age Movement anticipate the arrival of a Messiah, other than Jesus Christ, to save the world. This is based on a transition into a New World Order via a global religion and one-world economic system also called socialism or communism. Vehicles for this transition include the United Nations, the G7 (or G8), the European Union, and a proposed North American Union. In order to accomplish this transition, however, a form of global taxation must be instituted. In global bureaucratic language, a global tax is usually called a form of "innovative financing for development."

To make Americans into "global citizens," young people are told about the values of citizenship in the world and the United Nations through Model U.N. Programs in the schools.[31] They are not told about the role of communist spy and State Department official Alger Hiss in founding the U.N.

A more insidious approach involves the use of mind-altering drugs to break down the sense of one's self, creating "oneness" between an individual and his surroundings, including the world as a whole. A "consciousness researcher" by the name of Stephen Gray claims to have "deep insights into the spiritual effects of cannabis and how to work with marijuana through meditation." One author has written the article, "Cannabliss: The Spiritual Benefits of Marijuana." Another book is simply titled, *Cannabis and Spirituality.*

The use of drugs in some "religious" services can be used to facilitate "out-of-body" experiences and contacts with spirit beings and deities. Traditional Christians call these entities "demons" or evidence of Satan, however, and warn strongly against such practices.

For those who discount the influence of the New Age Movement, consider that Sally Quinn, who was married to former *Washington Post* executive editor Ben Bradlee until his death in 2014, writes about her belief in the occult in her book, *Finding Magic.* None of this was disclosed during the many years she was a member of the power elite and "Washington insider." Her book describes her belief in occultism, including using the ouija board, reading Tarot cards, consulting psychics, meeting LSD guru Timothy Leary, and casting a "hex" on somebody who then committed suicide.

S.J. Taylor writes in her book *Stalin's Apologist,* about *New York Times* Russia correspondent Walter Duranty, that Duranty and Satanist Aleister Crowley participated in drug-taking homosexual Satanic orgies. Crowley (1875-1947) described himself as the "Beast 666," or Antichrist, of the Book of Revelation. Some analysts say Crowley, who visited Russia twice (in 1898 and in 1913), was a mastermind of an international conspiracy rooted in Satanism, and that he helped the Communists in Russia and his philosophy played a role in the subsequent rise of the Nazis in Germany.

Our elites embrace the New Age. Jean Houston of the Foundation for Mind Research had tried to help Mrs. Clinton, when she was First Lady, "communicate" with Eleanor Roosevelt during a mystical "channeling" session. This kind of weirdness is typical of the New Age movement that backed Obama and will be a critical political force in 2018 and 2020. Though she favors the use of LSD in some settings to facilitate spirituality, there is no evidence Houston used the substance on Hillary Clinton during their meetings together. Houston, who has been working closely with the U.N. for decades, says, "There is a revolution going on! We're moving towards planetization within one century."

For those still "clinging" to their Bibles, as Obama once derisively referred to Christians, it is relevant to note that the Apostle Paul, a disciple and contemporary of Jesus Christ, condemned homosexual behavior as "against nature." [32] The deadly diseases that continue to wreak havoc on the gay community prove that he had a point and was correct, irrespective of the religious nature of his comments. The medical and scientific evidence can't be ignored.

As noted by Bible scholar William Barclay, Paul's remarks seemed, at first glance, like the work of "some almost hysterical moralist" at the time. But it was "an age of moral suicide," Barclay said, explaining that "Society from top to bottom was riddled with unnatural vice. Fourteen out of the first fifteen Roman Emperors were homosexuals."

We haven't reached that state of affairs in America quite yet. But we are approaching it. Obama, after all, was called by Andrew Sullivan in *Newsweek* magazine America's "first gay president." He should know. Sullivan, who is HIV-positive, was caught soliciting so-called "bare-backing sex" -- unprotected anal intercourse -- with other homosexuals.

This kind of moral degeneracy demonstrates that we are witnessing the transformation of America into a post-Christian society in which male-female differences are obliterated not only by the homosexual movement but by transgenderism. Sacred institutions such as the male-female relationship in marriage are seen as enemies of the revolution.

The National Lesbian & Gay Journalists Association now includes "transgendered" in its name, calling itself the Association of LGBTQ Journalists. It is funded by all of the big media organizations and instructs reporters on how to portray conservatives and Republicans as obstructing necessary social change. Fox News has been a financial backer for many years. In fact, Fox News personalities such as Guy Benson, Shepard Smith, and Tammy Bruce are openly homosexual. Benson also works for a "Christian" media organization called Salem Media Group.

In addition to these developments, there's far more of the Obama legacy that remains in place than Andrew Sullivan cares to admit. Obamacare, which was sold through the repeated lie that "If you like your health care plan, you can keep it," has not been repealed and if it is allowed to stay in place could lead to the rationing of health care and government decisions over life and death. Ione Whitlock of LifeTree, Inc., a pro-life group, has documented Soros support for what she calls the "Big Death" lobby, being implemented under the Obamacare legislation. The skyrocketing costs of health coverage under Obamacare are leading to a "death spiral" not only in the marketplace but in the lives of people.

So-called prison reform, which could release thousands of federal prisoners, many of whom are drug traffickers, has been a project financed by Soros for decades and was pushed by Obama. More recently, the libertarian Koch Brothers have poured millions of dollars into this cause as well. It found a sympathetic ear in the Trump White House from son-in-law Jared Kushner, an adviser to the president whose father served time in prison after pleading guilty to federal tax evasion, witness tampering, and other charges.

Indeed, acting on a plea from Kushner and reality TV star Kim Kardashian, Trump commuted the sentence of Alice Marie Johnson, a ringleader in a drug conspiracy that authorities described as the largest known drug operation in the history of Memphis, Tennessee. The conspiracy, linked to the Colombian Cali cartel, was characterized by so much violence and crime that the Obama Justice Department had never dared to recommend a commutation or pardon for her. The media had simply referred to her as "a first-time nonviolent offender."

In this regard, the Obama legacy lives on under Trump. On May 18, 2018, the Trump White House sponsored a summit on "prison reform" that included former top Obama official and "former" communist Van Jones. Jones was deeply involved in a Marxist group, Standing Together To Organize a Revolutionary Movement (STORM), which sent some of its members to Cuba for brainwashing. Jones would later become Obama's so-called Green Jobs Czar, only to resign when his communist background came to light. His career was financed by Soros.

Dr. Trent discovered that the Angela Davis group Critical Resistance had invented the "cop-watch concept" that would be popularized by Van Jones in

Oakland, California, through a group called Bay Area Police Watch. Davis, a communist, wrote, *Are Prisons Obsolete?*, a book arguing that criminals are victims of capitalist society.

Fortunately, Trump has pushed back against Obama's legacy on abortion. Obama was the first president to address Planned Parenthood, a major component of the abortion industry that was exposed for trafficking in aborted baby parts. His backer, billionaire Bill Gates, has poured tens of millions of dollars into the United Nations for population reduction measures.

The Abortion Industry

One of our ASI TV shows, "The Greatest Genocide Ever," links the ongoing death toll from abortion to the advent of Communism in Russia. It documents the number of abortions in the world, since the Russian Communist revolution legalized abortion, at 1 billion. Thomas Jacobson of the Global Life Campaign examined how the United Nations has become a leading proponent of abortion worldwide as a "human right." The U.N. Population Fund supported a one-child-per-family policy in communist China, which required forced abortions or sterilizations for women having a second child.

Globally, the Chinese Communist dictatorship is now the leader in death by abortion, with 381 million abortions and Russia at 256 million, while the U.S. has destroyed 60 million of the unborn since the infamous Roe v. Wade Supreme Court decision of 1973.

Inside the FBI under Obama, however, there was no interest in investigating Planned Parenthood. Indeed, we know that FBI attorney Lisa Page, who worked on the Clinton and Trump investigations, had said, "I truly hate these people," referring to pro-lifers attending the January 22, 2016, March for Life. This is how "diversity and inclusion" accommodates radical feminists and adulterers but not traditional Christians.

Sex Trafficking and Pornography

Under Obama, there wasn't one new federal indictment for violating obscenity laws. The last case, which was filed under the Bush presidency and prosecuted under Obama, involved obscene videos showing females engaging in sex acts involving human bodily waste and with animals. The pornographer, Ira Isaacs, was sentenced to serve 48 months in prison for engaging in the business of producing and selling obscene material.[33]

Research professor and author Dr. Judith Reisman told me on ASI TV that, in addition to the child pornography problem, child sex rings for the pleasure of pedophiles in Hollywood and elsewhere remain largely uninvestigated by the authorities. In her books, *Kinsey: Crimes & Consequences* and *Kinsey, Sex and Fraud,* Dr. Reisman explains how Alfred Kinsey, the father of the sexual revolution, was a pervert who knowingly used data from a Nazi pedophile in order to promote the idea that children were sexual beings.

Dr. Lori Handrahan has been documenting the scope of America's child porn industry and the involvement by America's national security and federal employees. During an appearance on ASI TV, she discussed such cases as former GOP House Speaker Dennis Hastert, who was exposed as a pedophile; and Jesse Loskarn, Chief of Staff for Senator Lamar Alexander, who was caught with child porn and killed himself.

It took the FBI more than a year to begin interviewing witnesses in the case of Lawrence G. Nassar, the former USA Gymnastics and Michigan State University doctor who was sentenced to prison for decades of sexual abuse involving more than 150 women and girls.

The facilitation of sex trafficking over the Internet through such sites as Backpage.com was effectively stopped when President Trump signed a bill to shut them down. [34] However, then-Rep. Frank Wolf had repeatedly urged the Obama Administration and Attorney General Eric Holder to close down the criminal enterprise. [35] In one letter to Holder, he said:

> When are you and your department going to get serious about solving this problem? How many more young girls are going to become victims before the department deals with this? From now on, I'm going to hold you

personally accountable for each victim trafficked on that Web site -- each someone's daughter, sister, or mother. I'm asking you -- not as attorney general but as a father -- to use your remaining time in office to find a way to end Backpage.com's trafficking of young girls and women.

Soros-funded organizations and publications such as *The Huffington Post* refer to some of these victims as "sex workers" and favor legalization of prostitution. Indeed, the Open Society Foundations has a project devoted to "sex worker rights." It supports the English Collective of Prostitutes in Britain and the Sex Workers Alliance in Ireland.

The Department of Justice on June 12, 2018, announced the arrest of more than 2,300 suspected online child sex offenders. The Internet Crimes Against Children (ICAC) task forces "identified 195 offenders who either produced child pornography or committed child sexual abuse, and 383 children who suffered recent, ongoing, or historical sexual abuse or production of child pornography," an official release said.

Nevertheless, the North American Man-Boy Love Association (NAMBLA) continues to operate a website openly. Homosexual activist David Thorstad, a member of the Socialist Workers Party, was a founding member and is featured on the web site, paying tribute to Harry Hay. "Harry was a vocal and courageous supporter of NAMBLA and intergenerational sexual relationships, though since his death many of the assimilationists in the gay and lesbian movement, including its most prominent organizations, have already sought to erase that part of his radicalism (not to mention his Communist roots and vocal critiques of their own accommodationist approach to the powers that be)," Thorstad declared.

The "powers that be" are those in government, corporations, and the media who conceal the communist nature of this movement.

Obama's Pornography Base

Obama had proclaimed homosexual activist Terry Bean, one of his top donors, as his "great friend and supporter." A co-founder of the major homosexual lobby, the Human Rights Campaign, Bean took a leave of absence from the group after he was arrested on charges involving sex with a minor. He tried to settle the case out of court, claimed innocence, and the charges were eventually dismissed. Bean chaired the Charles M. Holmes Foundation, which was named for homosexual pornographer Charles M. Holmes, a personal friend of Bean who died of AIDS and owned Falcon Studios, a producer of "high quality gay male videos." The *Huffington Post* defended Bean against charges he was a gay-porn kingpin.

Before the "Me Too" movement of sexual assault victims achieved prominence, my 1992 book, *The Playboy Foundation: A Mirror of the Culture?,* had documented how Playboy founder Hugh Hefner was abusing and exploiting women but was protected by the media and progressive groups because he paid them off -- to the tune of millions of dollars, through the Playboy Foundation and the "Hugh Hefner First Amendment Awards." The dirty secret was that Hefner and his daughter, Christie, who took over the company, were staunch Democrats. Hugh Hefner gave then-presidential candidate Barack Obama $2,300 in 2007, according to Federal Election Commission (FEC) records. Christie Hefner, who followed her father as chief executive officer of Playboy Enterprises, supported Obama's Senate run, contributing $1,500 to his campaign.

Former Playboy Playmate Miki Garcia testified before the Attorney General's Commission on Pornography in 1985, saying that Hefner encouraged Playmates to come to his mansion and "partake of the activities," including orgies and bisexual escapades. She said Playmates were forced to engage in sex acts with Hefner's associates through "peer pressure." As director of Playmate Promotions from 1976 to 1982, she said she was told by models "about rapes, mental and physical abuse, attempted murder, drug addiction, attempted suicide and prostitution."

Years later, the *Washington Post* would report that Bill Cosby, who would be convicted of drugging and sexually assaulting a woman at his home, had "partied with Hugh Hefner and was a regular at the magazine mogul's Playboy Mansion bacchanals," a term which means drunken orgies.

At the time that Hefner was financing the progressive movement, including drug legalization, there was no interest in exposing his exploitation of women. He had also financed the abortion rights movement, saying it kept women sexually available for men. That, too, was apparently just fine with the "women's movement."

This book will hopefully be remembered as prescient in terms of identifying and analyzing what Constance Cumbey has called "the hidden dangers of the rainbow." These forces are growing in strength. Various groups of "Rainbow People," some of them operating under the name Rainbow Family, have been gathering in National Forests since 1972 "to pray for peace on the planet." Police have made arrests for marijuana, DUI, disorderly conduct, and public nudity.

The Rainbow Nation

Analyst and author Trevor Loudon has written a series of articles, "The Rainbow Conspiracy," on the political aspects of this movement.[36] Loudon says the objective is to take the concept of Jesse Jackson's Rainbow Coalition and create a new American majority fusing communists, progressive whites, feminists, homosexuals, transgenders, minorities, Islamists and illegal immigrants. He discussed this at our November 10, 2017, conference in a YouTube and Roku video titled, "Obama's Plan for a One-Party Socialist State."

Loudon singles out Steve Phillips, author of *Brown is the New White,* as the key operative, who is working with Obama's approval. The left-wing group Democracy for America is promoting his book, saying, "The explosive population growth of people of color in America over the past fifty years has created the foundation for what Steve Phillips calls the 'New American Majority' -- 51% of the electorate, consisting of people of color (23 percent of all eligible voters) and white progressives (28 percent of all eligible voters). This majority is growing larger every day."

But this "New American Majority" also incorporates those with a secular, humanist, atheist, or New Age mentality. This coalition is indeed "growing larger every day" because of the breakdown in society and the destruction of traditional values. It grows in strength because of the "permanent revolution."

A vice chair of the Congressional Progressive Caucus, Rep. Jamie Raskin (D-Md.) is the leading humanist on Capitol Hill and has been described by the liberal press as having atheistic beliefs.

The "rainbow" strategy worked in 2008 and 2012 and could easily work again. Phillips has access to the resources of the Sandler Foundation, which has made grants exceeding $750 million, as a result of his marriage to its trustee Susan Sandler.

This approach seems to favor Democratic Senators such as Cory Booker and Kamala Harris as possible presidential candidates in 2020. Interestingly, both of them are black and support marijuana legalization. That position alone guarantees that millions of stoners, drawn from the millennial generation, may turn out to vote for them. They will vote for legal weed and then demand government help when their mental facilities deteriorate. According to government statistics, marijuana is the most commonly used illicit drug. The estimate is that 22.2 million people have used it in the past month. They are a potential major voting bloc.

The 1991 book, appropriately titled, *Rainbow Nation Without Borders: Toward an Ecotopian Millennium,* confirms what Constance Cumbey warned people about and takes Trevor Loudon's analysis to a global level. The author, Alberto Ruz Buenfil, an "international networker" and "social change" activist from Mexico, discusses an "Aquarian Conspiracy" designed to bring about "a shift in human consciousness." He explains that the "conspirators" believe the present Christian era is coming to an end and that a new millennium "will come about when science, art, ecology, and spirit unite with traditional wisdom to create a universal science of being…"

Interestingly, Alberto Ruz Buenfil cites the "messianic crusade" behind Jesse Jackson's Rainbow Coalition as an example for the United States to follow. He also highlighted "major world changes such as the Russian perestroika and glasnost directed by another charismatic figure, Mikhail Gorbachev." The concepts of perestroika and glasnost were designed to convince the West that communism was dead. Gorbachev, the former Soviet president, had declared his commitment to a one-world communist state, saying on November 2, 1987, "We are moving towards a new world, the world of communism. We shall never turn off that road."

This leads us to Robert Muller, a U.N. veteran who had served as assistant to U.N. Secretary-General U Thant, a Buddhist. He wrote *New Genesis: Shaping a Global Spirituality.* "His thesis was that underlying conflicts between nations were often religious conflicts and that the mystical experience of unity was the antidote to fundamentalism," said Rick Doblin of MAPS. "He thought we needed to bring the mystics of the different religions together to teach peace."

Obama and Farrakhan

Obama's debt to the Nation of Islam's Louis Farrakhan is another scandal that was concealed. We now know that this relationship was covered-up for 13 years, only to surface publicly in 2018 when a photograph of Obama and Farrakhan together was published. It came out that Farrakhan's organization was involved in Obama's campaign for the state Senate in Illinois before he ran for president. Askia Muhammad, former head of the Washington office of the Nation of Islam's official newspaper, *The Final Call,* said that a "staff member" for the Congressional Black Caucus contacted him "sort of in a panic" after he took the photo at a meeting in 2005. This led to the cover-up.

Dubbed "Black America's most controversial and popular Muslim" by his *Final Call* newspaper, Farrakhan is a black separatist and anti-Semite who blames the white man for black problems and was a friend of anti-American regimes in Iran and Cuba. A fan of Paul Robeson, the secret Communist Party member, Farrakhan had praised killer Winnie Mandela, dubbed the "Mother" of the "Rainbow Nation" of South Africa.

The Nation of Islam believes white people were created by a mad scientist named Yakub and constitute an inferior race of people. The movement has its own interpretation of Islam and was founded by Elijah Muhammad, who wrote, *The Fall of America,* in which he talked about the "Mother Plane" or "wheel" -- a flying saucer -- being a message from God.

Once again, however, we had the truth in advance, as conservative black businessman Zubi Diamond said at an America's Survival, Inc. conference back in 2011, "Barack Obama is Louis Farrakhan and Karl Marx rolled into one." It was a statement proven true by events.

With Obama out of office, our task takes on new urgency, as an effort is underway to make Obama into a cult-like figure who still cannot be challenged or exposed.

The Challenge Ahead

Of the literally dozen or so pro-Obama books written over the years, the pro-Obama *Washington Post* reviewed two of them, saying, "The early drafts of the Obama legacy are in -- and they're way over the top." The paper explained, "They read almost as synchronized in their sympathy, methodically reciting Obama's achievements and minimizing his reversals."

We can expect more of this. Barack and Michelle Obama have a joint book deal worth $65 million and have "entered into a multi-year agreement to produce films and series with Netflix," the internet-based entertainment service. "The Obamas will produce a diverse mix of content, including the potential for scripted series, unscripted series, docu-series, documentaries and features. These projects will be available to the 125 million member Netflix households in 190 countries," said a Netflix press release. Reports indicated the deal was worth $50 million to the Obamas and was arranged by Ted Sarandos, a major campaign contributor for Obama and the streaming giant's creative-content chief who oversees an $8 billion budget.[37]

Meanwhile, Obama's presidential center planned for Chicago, Illinois, was caught in an institutional "bait and switch" in a land grab of park space. The *American Thinker's* Thomas Lifson, whose journalism was cited as backup in a lawsuit on this matter, noted that the original plan was for a federal entity to take possession of the land and build an Obama Presidential Library, which would be publicly owned and controlled. "That was the bait used to obtain priceless open park land that would be taken away from the citizens of Chicago," he wrote. "The switch came when the presidential library plan was sidelined, and in its place was instituted a 'presidential center' that would be under the control of a private foundation, with Barack Obama himself in a position to shape the center's planning, mission, and operations toward whatever ends he desires." [38]

Rather than being an academic-type institution, it appears that the new Obama presidential center will be the focus of "community organizing." Obama says, "If I could do that effectively, then I would create a hundred, or a thousand, or a million young Barack Obamas or Michelle Obamas."

As a former president, Obama is already doing "community organizing" on a global scale. He traveled to Germany to meet with Angela Merkel, visited with Bill and Melinda Gates at a pro-U.N. "Goalkeepers" conference, and went to Canada for a major progressive conference, under the sponsorship of the group Canada 2020, closely tied to Justin Trudeau and the Liberal Party. Then Obama went to Communist China, where he and President Xi were photographed smiling and drinking tea at a state guesthouse in Beijing. They were labeled "veteran cadres," a term that refers to experienced Communist operatives.

Equally significant, Obama is being lionized to the point of deification. The Obama name is being put on schools, libraries, streets, and highways across the United States. Barack Obama's birthday has been declared an Illinois holiday. Obama is being transformed into a cultural icon and even mystical historical figure. The media-entertainment complex has declared its fondness for the Obama presidency, with "Saturday Night Live" featuring Chance the Rapper belting out a few musical numbers including "Come Back Barack." Author and writer Matt Margolis predicts an effort to put Obama's likeness on U.S. currency.

But if we look back and examine his proclamations, we begin to grasp that his state of mind bordered on lunacy. "We are the ones we have been waiting for," he had proclaimed during his presidential campaign. Mental health expert J.D. Mitschke said on America's Survival TV that Obama seems like a "messianic narcissist." Mitschke, author of *Modern-Day Liberalism: Exploring the Psychological Foundations of the Disorder,* highlights Obama's repeated use of "I" or "me" in his pronouncements and his bald-faced lies on matters like health care in order to sell socialized medicine.

David L. Scheiner, M.D., had claimed in 2008 that "Senator Barack Obama is in overall good physical and mental health needed to maintain the resiliency required in the Office of President." But Obama did not release any medical or mental health records and did not make his doctors available to the media.

Under Trump, however, a firm founded by two of Obama's senior campaign architects, Julianna Smoot and Paul Tewes, arranged a discussion at the National Press Club to kick off Mental Health Awareness Month by highlighting his alleged mental unfitness for the presidency.

Former Romanian intelligence chief Lt. Gen. Ion Mihai Pacepa, the highest-ranking Soviet bloc intelligence official ever to defect to the West, told America's Survival, Inc.:

> May God forgive me for comparing Barack Obama with Romania's Marxist tyrant Nicolae Ceausescu, but President Obama gave me the feeling of seeing Ceausescu's ghost on our shores. "We are the ones we have been waiting for," Barack Obama proclaimed during his presidential campaign. An indiscrete YouTube sequence published by Fox TV showed the picture of communist idol Che Guevara hanging on the wall in his campaign office. The Democratic Party put the icing on the cake, proclaiming Obama an American Messiah. Obama agreed. He stated that the beginning of his presidency would be "the moment when the rise of the oceans began to slow and our planet began to heal." Some Americans regarded Obama's rhetoric as millennial generation talk. For me, it was thinly veiled "Ceausism." "A man like me is born once every five hundred years,"

was Ceausescu's version. He also kept a picture of Che in his office.

Moral Bankruptcy

In the face of this unprecdented assault on the nation's moral fabric, the 2018 Conservative Political Action Conference (CPAC) banned the pro-family group MassResistance from even paying for an exhibit table. The scandal unfolded in the wake of the year's previous scandal, when CPAC in 2017 invited -- and then disinvited -- so-called "gay conservative" Milo Yiannopoulos, an editor of Breitbart, after he made comments condoning man-boy sex.

As someone who met President Reagan in the White House and heard his speeches at CPAC, I have the experience and history in the movement to comment on the dangerous direction taken by the organizers. I introduced then-Rep. Mike Pence at CPAC in 2009. My group America's Survival, Inc. had been an exhibitor at CPAC in the past.

Ronald Reagan would be rolling over in his grave if he knew what the leadership of the American Conservative Union (ACU) was doing to the conservative movement. The ACU, which sponsors the Conservative Political Action Conference, has destroyed one leg of Reagan's "three-legged stool" approach to conservatism.

Reagan's approach emphasized the fiscal/economic, social/moral, and national security aspects of conservatism. Under this approach, the secret of success is maintaining all three legs of the stool.

ACU executive director Dan Schneider, who claims to be an Eagle Scout, banned MassResistance from even having a table in the exhibit hall, saying he was offended by president Brian Camenker's alleged disrespectful tone toward gays during a speech from years ago. Meanwhile, the so-called Log Cabin Republicans, who march in gay rights parades and hold graphic and obscene signs, were allowed to have a booth in the exhibit hall. They promote gay marriage and "trans troops."

In another controversy, CPAC abandoned the Ronald and Nancy Reagan stance against using illegal drugs and in 2018 featured a "debate" on the subject with somebody from the Colorado Cannabis Chamber of Commerce. The use of marijuana in Colorado has destroyed the minds of many young people, leading to more fatalities on the road, more homelessness, and even murders. One of the most notorious was a Denver man, Richard Kirk, who pleaded guilty to killing his wife while he was high on marijuana edibles. Kirk was sentenced to 30 years in prison.

As the bodies of the stoners and their victims were piling up, Republican Senator Cory Gardner of Colorado emerged as one of Big Marijuana's biggest friends in Washington, D.C. So have the libertarian billionaire Koch Brothers. They denounced Attorney General Jeff Sessions' rollback of former President Obama's illegal pro-marijuana policies. [39]

When Gardner joined with Democratic Senator Elizabeth Warren (D-Mass.) to introduce a bill that would shield the marijuana industry from enforcement of federal law, he claimed he had President Trump's support. The National Narcotics Officer's Associations' Coalition (NNOAC) responded by asking President Trump not to weaken the federal policy on marijuana. Drug policy expert David Evans has appealed to Trump not to cave to the marijuana industry and its political allies, saying he is alarmed by Jared Kushner's financial ties to George Soros and Peter Thiel, another billionaire with investments in the marijuana business. [40] Thiel, a homosexual, was a featured speaker at the Republican national convention in 2016.

Liberal Judges

The courts are an area in which liberal judicial appointees, many appointed by Obama, continue to exert major influence, including in transgenderism.

The late Phyllis Schlafly's book, *The Supremacists: The Tyranny of Judges and How to Stop It,* listed many examples of how judges have rewritten the Constitution and how they have:

- Censored the Pledge of Allegiance in public schools.
- Removed the Ten Commandments from public schools, buildings, and parks.
- Declared an unrestricted right to abortion at any time during the entire nine months of

pregnancy, taking a legislative function away from the state legislatures and imposing a judicial fiat without any textual basis in the U.S. Constitution.

- Changed the definition of marriage.
- Banned the acknowledgment of God in public schools, at graduations, and at football games.
- Imposed taxes and spending of taxpayers' money.
- Rewritten laws of criminal procedures.
- Dismantled laws that protect internal security, and
- Upheld racial preferences and quotas in hiring and college admissions.

In a case decided by the U.S. Court of Appeals for the 3rd Circuit in *Doe v. Boyertown Area School District*, liberal judges ruled that a school can open its locker rooms, showers, and restrooms to students of the opposite sex. The group Alliance Defending Freedom is representing students in the case concerned about their privacy rights and privacy protections.

The Fourth Circuit ruling against the Peace Cross memorial in Maryland is another abomination. This historic cross-shaped Veterans Memorial, which has stood since 1925 in honor of 49 Maryland men who died during WWI, has been ordered destroyed by a court packed with Obama appointees. The First Liberty Institute has intervened in the case on behalf of The American Legion whose seal is prominently displayed at the memorial's center. The case against the cross was brought by the atheist and progressive American Humanist Association.

What we are witnessing is a full-blown war on Christianity and traditional Christian moral values that accelerated under Obama. Even at Bible-based Wellesley College (Hillary Clinton's alma mater), we see evidence of the transformation. Its Wellesley Magazine published an article (Winter 2018), "How to Raise a Feminist Boy," written by a lesbian graduate of Wellesley.

The ruling in the Peace Cross case and many others demonstrates how the courts bear much responsibility for America's moral decline. Obama did not start these trends, but packing the courts with "progressives" during the eight years of his presidency accelerated the anti-Christian rulings.

In regard to previous decisions banning prayer and Bible readings from the public schools, Christian prayer has been replaced in many cases by Eastern-style religious practices. Even more ominous, a group called the Satanic Temple is sponsoring "After School Satan Clubs" in the public schools.

In order to save America from these gathering forces of Marxism, radical Islam, and the New Age, it is necessary to investigate the forces trying to overthrow the Trump presidency or force him from office. A group of prominent conservatives and Catholic activists sent a letter to President Trump in 2017 seeking an investigation of collusion between the

Obama Administration, the Vatican, the United Nations, and the George Soros-funded progressive forces. [41] In an interview about this on ASI TV, Elizabeth Yore, one of the signers, discussed one aspect, the "unholy alliance between the Vatican and the United Nations," by focusing critical attention on Vatican adviser Professor Jeffrey Sachs, a global tax advocate in favor of population control measures.

Obama's "Collusion" Scandal

The letter asks whether a Vatican "regime change" was engineered by the Obama administration, with the support of George Soros, to replace Pope Benedict with Francis.[42] Yore tells me, "I'm convinced that if the Obama Administration was spying and interfering in the Trump campaign, they would certainly move heaven and earth (pun intended) to get rid of Benedict who would not have supported the Muslim migration into Europe." Benedict was evicted and made into a "Pope Emeritus" after the fallout from a speech at the University of Regensburg in which he noted the violent tendencies in Islam and called for Christianity to take a stand.

The controversy took on added significance when Marcantonio Colonna, in his 2018 book, *The Dictator Pope,* suggested that Francis may have diverted Church funds to support Hillary Clinton's failed presidential campaign. He said this claim "has been repeatedly rumored from reliable sources," and that verification "could be the unraveling of an enormous scandal."

The Obama Administration's intervention in Vatican affairs would not be surprising. It had clearly intervened to destroy Canada's conservative government in 2015. Obama's intervention helped elect a pro-abortion Catholic, Justin Trudeau, who ran on a platform to legalize marijuana and establish more injection sites for heroin users around the country.[43] Obama had tried, but failed, to defeat Israeli Prime Minister Benjamin Netanyahu.

At the current time, Trump is still fighting for his own political survival against the Deep State. "This is a battle for the soul of the United States of America," says Elizabeth Yore.

## From Oprah to Obama and Beyond

By Constance Cumbey

David Letterman used his famous top 10 list to entertain his late night show audience. Oprah was a favorite subject for gathering laughs. One night he used this one:

> Top Ten Things Columbus Would Say About America If He Were Alive Today: No. 6: "How did you come to choose the leader you call Oprah?"[44]

Many laughs were generated by this. There were once equally hilarious jokes about somebody named Donald Trump being President. But it became reality.

Suddenly, given the unexpected becoming reality in American life, even the prospect of flamboyant New Age media queen Oprah becoming president is no longer funny nor unbelievable. Trump was taken as a joke by some and regarded by others as a candidate who could not "insult his way to the presidency." Oprah Winfrey has enjoyed a cult-like following of New Age activists, bored housewives, those admiring her financial success, and wannabe authors who want Oprah's blessings for their books. Many famed household name personalities owe their fame and career to Oprah Winfrey. Some of the best known include Dr. Oz and Dr. Phil. The name given to this was "The Oprah Effect."[45]

According to Oprah Winfrey's latest Wikipedia account, "[S]everal assessments rank her as the most influential woman in the world." A special issue of Time magazine, "Women Changing the World," featured Winfrey. She was host of "The Oprah Winfrey Show" for 25 years and currently serves as Chairman and CEO of OWN: Oprah Winfrey Network. She is the founder of O, The Oprah Magazine and oversees Harpo Films.

When she delivered a keynote address on May 11, 2018 at the University of Southern California (USC) Annenberg School for Communication and Journalism, home of the USC Center on Public Diplomacy, she was described by Dean Willow Bay as "arguably one of America's most beloved public diplomats" and "the ideal role model to address our graduates."

"Opinionated," "bombastic" and "flamboyant" are words descriptive of Oprah Winfrey. The word "ebullient" might be another. So are "powerful" and "complex." "New Age," "narcissistic," "controlling" and "insecure." All these are words used by those knowing her best to describe her. Some of those using the more pejorative terms of "narcissistic" and even "lying" include members of her own immediate and extended family. [46]

Winfrey's speech accepting the Cecil B. DeMille lifetime achievement award at the Golden Globes led to speculation that she would run for president in 2020. During its broadcast, the official NBC Twitter page posted an intriguing tweet showing a laughing image of Oprah Winfrey with the message: "Nothing but respect for OUR future president."

Richard Greene, a contributor to *The Huffington Post*, endorsed Oprah for president, saying, "America is a heavily religious/spiritual country and Oprah Winfrey is genuinely and deeply spiritual." While she is not an overtly religious "Christian," he said that "in the history of our nation, and perhaps any nation, there has never been an Oprah Winfrey. She is a national treasure, one of the greatest communicators in history and a gift to our nation and the world. And if she chooses to do so, Oprah Winfrey is absolutely ready to bring her gifts to 1600 Pennsylvania Avenue." (Note: *The Huffington Post*, a platform for advocates of abortion and homosexual rights and marijuana legalization, was named after Arianna Huffington's ex-husband, Michael Huffington, who was born rich and then turned gay. She used his money from a divorce settlement to start the on-line news service in 2005. Arianna, like Oprah, is very influential in New Age circles and has been described as an ordained "Minister Of Light" in the cult headed by the late John-Roger and known as the Movement For Spiritual Inner Awareness.)

If Oprah did run, rumors about her personal life and why she is still unmarried would inevitably be raised. Oprah is herself credited with featuring LGBTQ journalist Greg Brock on the first "National Coming Out Day" for homosexuals on her syndicated television talk show back in 1988. [47]

How did Oprah gain her fanatical following? If she decided to be a presidential aspirant, could she possibly be successful? If not, will she continue to play the political kingmaker role she has enjoyed since she blessed Obama?

Clearly, the Obama presidency owed much to Oprah. She was the first major voice to suggest that she would like to see Obama run for president. She was also a major source of his fundraising. [48] It appears obvious that his major opponent, the then-favored candidate Hillary Clinton, lost support from influential New Age backers because Oprah had blessed Obama's candidacy.[49] She was rewarded in 2013 by Obama hanging the Presidential Medal of Freedom around her neck. Equally clearly, Hillary Clinton, who had courted New Age support during her husband's eight years of White House tenancy, may well have lost the Democratic nomination for the same reasons.

Whether Winfrey runs for president or not, the New Age Movement is still a major and growing force. I have documented the rise of this movement in my book, *The Hidden Dangers of the Rainbow: The New Age Movement and Our Coming Age of Barbarism*. My book points out that its "toolbox is mysticism," or "altered states of consciousness," which are said to draw people into a relationship with spiritual forces in the world that are part of a "New World Order" and global religion to be headed by an anticipated "messianic figure" of some kind. A state of mind favorable to such a development can result from mind-control techniques exercised by cult leaders, meditation, or drugs. There are so many cults today that experts exist to "deprogram" their members and recruits.

An Opening for Oprah

Marilyn Ferguson's 1980 book, *The Aquarian Conspiracy*, was the first book to describe in detail a powerful network of organizations and personalities working to bring about radical cultural and social change in the United States and the world through the "expansion of consciousness." She quoted with approval other observers watching some components of the New Age Movement and describing them as being a "political/spiritual entity."

But Oprah took this movement to a new level. In 2009, according to the book *Stealing Fire*, Oprah and "spiritual teacher" Eckhart Tolle teamed up for a 10-part online video series *Oprah & Eckhart Tolle: A New Earth*, with 11 million people from 129 countries watching. [50] This was said to be more than the size of the crowd which greeted the pope's visit to New York City and 9 million more than the largest Islamic pilgrimage to Mecca. It was later presented on television. Tolle claims to be in a state of oneness with the universe and in near constant bliss.

In my view, this movement, global in scope, may now be even more influential than international communism and radical Islam. In fact, the New Age movement may play more of a role than the other anti-American forces in the world today in undermining our Judeo-Christian culture and traditions. Quoting Marilyn Ferguson's *Aquarian Conspiracy* (page 410), we read:

> These social movements transcend traditional national borders, with Germans joining French demonstrators to protest nuclear power plants. Johann Quanier, British publisher of The New Humanity Journal, said, "The strands of free thinking within Europe are now being drawn together; despite the conflicts, the tension, and the differences, that territory is preeminently suitable for the emergence of the new political-spiritual framework."

Indeed, the New Age dream is not limited to Europe. It is a global dream they share to the extent of their "level of initiation" into New Age theologies and ideologies. It is one of "a political-spiritual framework" that can be found in movements for global governance, the United Nations, and the European Union.

There is some debate among Protestants and even traditionalist Catholics as to whether Pope Francis -- or another pope -- could become a "False Prophet" or New Age "Messiah." His reported alleged statements on homosexuality being "God-given" and "there is no Hell" have triggered some of that chatter. [51] Critics of Francis, the first Jesuit pope, note his sympathy for mysticism in his environmental encyclical, *Laudato si*, which cites the work of Teilhard De Chardin, who was nearly excommunicated. De Chardin was described by Wallace Johnson, the author of *The Death Of Evolution*, as "a bridge between Christians and Marxists." He notes that, in a letter dated January 26, 1936, Teilhard wrote: "What increasingly dominates my interest... is the effort to establish within myself, and to diffuse around me, a new religion (let's call it an improved Christianity if you like) whose personal god is no longer the great neolithic landowner of times gone by, but the soul of the world..." This is an expression of New Age philosophy.

The words of Teilhard De Chardin, who tried to combine the theory of evolution with the Christian faith, are featured on a wall at the Intercultural Center at (Jesuit) Georgetown University: "The Age of Nations is past. The task before us now, if we would not perish, is to build the Earth."

What's more, Catholic observers such as Matt Gaspers of Catholic Family News have appeared on ASI TV to assert that Pope Francis has come down on the side of the "progressive," and even Marxist, forces in the world today. In another interview on America's Survival TV, George Neumayr, author of *The Political Pope*, examined the Marxist ideology driving Francis and his seeming indifference to the threats posed by radical Islam and Russian communism. Russia continues to be a country with special significance in terms of the Fatima revelations and Bible prophecy. At the same time, the Vatican's increasingly cozy relationship with the Chinese

Communist regime has been criticized. Bishop Marcelo Sanchez Sorondo, the chancellor of the Pontifical Academy of Social Sciences, has said that China is exercising "the social doctrine" of the church.

It is my observation that the New Age Movement has moved with great dexterity in a variety of religious circles. It appears that virtually all churches and religious groups have been infiltrated to some degree with mysticism and "evolutionary" type beliefs. This leaves those with such views from church to church, sect to sect, with a commonality they did not find before. Then they have the problem of the remaining "fundamentalists", "orthodox", and "traditionalists" within those groups who stand in the way of the "New World Order."

New Age true believers are also in the process of executing what they call "The Armageddon Script." That was the title of a prominent New Age book by English New Ager (also a Church organist!) Peter Lemesurier. He detailed a fantastic effort that would culminate in rejoicing followers dressed in shining white following their new Messiah from the Mt. of Olives. They would be, not as much religious, but a rite to appease the various archetypal expectations of many with the staging of a fake apocalypse. Their cause would be embraced by all segments of society ranging from atheists to occultists. The "massed forces of the Old Age" could be disregarded. They would go on to destroy each other in a massive, mutual venting of "long pent up aggression."[52]

One of the boldest books announcing New Age plans and strategies, his *Armageddon Script* was released before the New Agers believed themselves to have serious opposition – in 1981. One of Lemesurier's publishers was none other than Findhorn, a group "guided by the inner voice of spirit, where we work in co-creation with the intelligence of nature and take inspired action towards our vision of a better world," and operating through its then Thule Press.[53]

In my speech to the November 10, 2017, America's Survival conference, I explained how the goal of the New Age Movement is to overthrow what they call "Peoples of the Book" – all monotheistic religions (Jews, Christians, and Moslems) in general and Christian civilization in particular. That New Age Movement has functioned, as explained by Marilyn Ferguson, the pivotal New Age chronicler, as operating through what they call a SPIN (Segmented, polycentric, integrated networks). It operates, per Ferguson, like a badly noded fishnet, where if there is a problem and something is lost, they close ranks without it, the fishnet is mended, and they go on as if it had not existed. This is exactly what they tried to do with Jim Jones and his Jonestown – a New Age socialist experiment that crashed badly and ended in a revolutionary suicide of hundreds dead. They calmly ascribed what happened to fundamentalist Christianity, knowing full well within their ranks that Jones had been an ardent activist maintaining a New Age center the entire time.[54]

I used my time at this conference to explain the significance of a powerful European politician -- of whom most Americans are surprisingly unaware -- Javier Solana. His full name is Javier Solana de Madariaga. He is a Spanish politician and American-educated physics professor who had been a leader in the left-wing anti-Vietnam War activities of the late 1960s and considered by many to be anti-American and subversive.

Solana was closely related to and mentored by Salvador de Madariaga, a leader in the critical area of "global governance." Salvador de Madariaga was considered so anti-Christian that he would not permit his two daughters to be baptized. When Mexico persecuted its Christian community, starting with the Catholics, there were moves to keep Mexico out of the League of Nations. It was Salvador de Madariaga's impassioned speech to the League that resulted in Mexico's admission at the peak of that bloody war against Mexican Christianity. (Note: the film, "For Greater Glory: The True Story of Cristiada," concerned the Mexican government's anti-Christian campaign.)

American conservatives and the Spanish population alike were startled when Javier Solana was suddenly in late 1995 named the new head of NATO and was given sole authority to make the bombing decisions over Yugoslavia in the Kosovo conflict. It was the Clinton administration that gave Javier Solana his extreme clout in global governance circles by handing him NATO to run. Not only did he run it with more clout than his predecessors and successors, he was given powers no other NATO head has ever had – to make the sole decisions on whether to employ bombs. This was given him on January 30, 1999, with the cooperation of Kofi Annan of the United Nations, and all NATO countries agreeing to the proposal.

Solana bragged of this in a late winter speech in the U.S. that he had been given that authority. He told them that "I don't intend to use that authority without checking in with the others, but nevertheless, the power is mine and mine alone."[55] It is this kind of power that is being reserved for a New Age world leader who may still be in the process of being groomed.

The Spanish population was particularly surprised because a major Solana claim to fame in Spain was his anti-NATO cries of "We are RADICALLY opposed to Spain's entry into NATO." Canadians were surprised as well. Javier Solana had dispatched three Spanish warships against Canada in what had almost been a shooting war at high sea between Spain and Canada over fishing rights.

Under his leadership, Javier Solana expanded NATO beyond its traditional role as anti-communist alliance, increased its membership by many countries, and worked closely with Russia. In 1999, as the High Representative designate of the European Union For Common Foreign and Security Policy, he engineered a "strategic partnership" between the European Union and Russia.

In my talk to America's Survival, I emphasized the important role in the direction of first "European" and then "global" unity. They call it "global governance," which they say is best achieved by "thinking globally, acting locally." Cliff's two books on the U.N., *Global Bondage* and *Global Taxes for World Government*, explain many of the governmental forces at work on the global level to bring this about.

Solana's mentor, Salvador de Madariaga, had deep involvement in the area of "global governance," as well as Sufi mysticism and Theosophy. [56] One typically finds links between the occult and globalist figures.

The Theosophical Society, a powerful global force, was formed in New York City in 1875 by a trio of occult believers – Helena Petrovna Blavatsky, Colonel Henry Steel Olcott, and William Q. Judge. They believed they were in contact with visible to them "spiritual forces" aka "The Masters of Wisdom." They enlisted many rich and famous in their cause which was to prepare the world to receive a new "messiah." They had a candidate identified for that position starting in 1910 – a young Indian man named Jiddu Krishnamurti. He would, they believed, lead the world into a New World Order that would include a New World Religion." [57] That "New World Religion" would be a pantheistic type of incorporation of mystical elements of existing world religions, combining believers to seek "continued revelation" as they are "initiated" into the mysteries of deepest occultism.

In addition to featuring my remarks at its November 10, 2017, National Press Club conference, America's Survival comments regularly on the influence of various New Age organizations in its newsletter. ASI is one of the few conservative groups which seem to take the New Age seriously. In his youth, Cliff Kincaid did personal research on the topic, visiting several New Age or Eastern religious-style communes such as New Vrindaban in West Virginia, a Hare Krishna community, the Parapsychology laboratory at Duke University, and the Edgar Cayce Association for Research and Enlightenment at Virginia Beach, Virginia. Later, during a trip to Colorado he witnessed a packed gathering of supporters of "Her Holiness Sai Maa," described as "a world-renowned spiritual master, healer, and humanitarian" [58] who claims a doctorate in spirituality from the Open International University. Her audience consisted of ordinary Americans desperately looking for meaning in life.

In regard to the Obama connection to these groups and the overall network, ASI noted:

> The "former" Communist and Obama Administration official Van Jones spoke at the Interfaith Visionary Call To Action Conference on Sustainable Development held on October 19, 2010, and sponsored by the Temple of Understanding (TOU), another important New Age group. A Non-Governmental Organization (NGO) in Consultative Status with the UN Economic and Social Council, the TOU describes itself

as "an active member of the NGO community working on the inside of the United Nations to advance social justice."

Another powerful New Age group working through the U.N. is World Goodwill, a project of the Lucis Trust. Its original publishing house was named Lucifer Publishing and was changed in 1924 to "Lucis Publishing." Cliff Kincaid visited the headquarters of World Goodwill, noting books on the shelves that included several by Blavatsky, Mikhail Gorbachev, and the influential *The Coming of the Cosmic Christ* by Matthew Fox. A United Nations flag greets visitors.

I have personally kept tabs on Fox since the beginning of my research in 1981. He was born as Timothy Fox and Matthew was the name he adopted when he entered the Roman Catholic priesthood. He wreaked much damage across the board in theological circles. His influence was felt across the entirety of the New Age Movement. Fox was subsequently excommunicated as a Roman Catholic priest in 1993. His current website proclaims Fox to be "bearing witness for social, environmental, and gender justice…" and claims he is preparing five books for publication.

The United Nations maintains an official "Meditation Room" in the U.N. building where officials gather to achieve what they call cosmic consciousness. Cliff Kincaid visited and was photographed in this strange room. The U.N.'s brand of religion can also be seen in the fact that a few blocks from the U.N. is the

Quest Book Shop, where U.N. officials also gather to meditate. The bookstore's website advertises gift items that include "a large selection of Tarot decks, one of the best selections of incense in the New York City, candles, semi-precious gemstones, mala beads, greeting cards, statues, essential oils, Tibetan singing bowls, pendulums, bells, Yoga mats and bags, meditation cushions, feng shui crystals, runestones, and more." (A similar place can be found in Alexandria, Virginia, just outside of Washington, D.C., called "Sacred Circle.")

The U.N. Environmental Program once promoted the idea of an "Environmental Sabbath," encouraging children to hold hands around a tree and meditate.

Gods for a New Age

A few New Age cults and their leaders have received major media attention. Unfortunately, they appear to be few and far between. The Jim Jones People's Temple cult was often mischaracterized as "Christian fundamentalism" rather than the mass Marxist-Socialist-New Age venture that it truly was. Other New Age cults that have from time to time come under the public critical eye have included the Sweat Lodge of James Arthur Ray[59]; the Heaven's Gate UFO cult of Marshall Applewhite[60]; the Order of the Solar Temple (French suicide cult); Bhagwan Shree Rajneesh and his attempted Oregon takeover replete with chemical attacks and the poisoning of opponents; and Ira Einhorn, a former "peace activist" and Earth Day leader convicted of killing his girlfriend. Einhorn had been the master of ceremonies at the first Earth Day rally on April 22, 1970. [61]

Probably the largest New Age cult to receive major media attention in recent times is Scientology. HBO ran a documentary, "Going Clear," about the cult on March 20, 2015, focusing on Scientology influence in Hollywood, mostly through actors like Tom Cruise and John Travolta. Former Scientologist Leah Remini has done a yeoman's job of educating the public on the cult.

However, several alleged sex cults are reported to be operating In Hollywood as well. A "self-help" organization called Nxivm has been labeled a cult and accused of involvement in sex trafficking. The group denies the charges and affirms that NXIVM is a company "whose mission is to raise human awareness, foster an ethical humanitarian civilization, and celebrate what it means to be human." [62]

One of Cliff's newsletters looked at the tragic case of the prominent LGBT Hart family, including two lesbian "moms," Jennifer and Sarah Hart, and their six adopted children, who died when their car went over a California cliff in March of 2018. Police confirmed the lesbian driver was drunk, and deliberately drove her family to their deaths. Some of their children who died were sedated. Some of the kids had previously reported being abused, with one asking a neighbor for food. The *Oregonian* reported, "The Hart family was a regular at Oregon's earthy festivals and shows, according to Zippy Lomax, who met them in 2012 at the annual Beloved festival in

Tidewater [Oregon] that celebrates art, mysticism, music and yoga."

New Age festivals are supposed to be about finding "God." But *High Times* magazine features them on its list of places to be. One of the sponsors of one such event, the Beloved festival in Oregon, was a marijuana business offering "top grade tasty cannabis." This is worrisome because in her "Declaration of a State of War," Weather Underground terrorist Bernardine Dohrn had declared, "We fight in many ways. Dope is one of our weapons." Libertarians have their own version of the New Age, advertised as Porcupine Freedom Festivals, or PorcFest, with marijuana use rampant.

Most of the activities at these festivals might be considered to be harmless. But careful observers should be reminded of the so-called 60s' Love generation, which took an ominous turn and culminated in the Manson Family massacre in 1969. Charles Manson had taken a group of young people, subjected them to heavy drug use in a commune-type setting, and ordered them to commit mass murder. Bernardine Dohrn, the future Obama backer, had praised the followers of mass murderer Charles Manson and designated Manson himself as a "true revolutionary."

The Russian Connection

What's more, there is a "bridge" to the movement that also is Russian in nature. Barbara Marx Hubbard bragged in a 1988 Seattle Unity Church speech that "from the top to the bottom, the entire Soviet leadership had made the 'Quantum Leap.'" She claimed that they had made an "end run around national sovereignty" and that Russia would lead the world into this "New Age."

Of historical interest, there were clear Russian connections to the very founding of the modern New Age Movement. New Agers publicly have proclaimed "Theosophy" as its "Mother Ship," and its founder, Madame Helena Petrovna Blavatsky, was the daughter of a Russian princess. She wrote several books and lengthy journals that included the New Age landmark pieces *The Secret Doctrine* and *ISIS Unveiled.* The scholarly paper, "The Occult Revival in Russia Today and Its Impact on Literature," describes how "post-Soviet Russia" has embraced New Age and occult ideas, even what the author, German academic Birgit Menzel, calls "dark" or "evil forces." [63]

Former KGB officer Konstantin Preobrazhensky has called the Russian Orthodox Church "Putin's Espionage Church," referring to the Russian President and former KGB officer, and devotes a major portion of his book, *KGB/FSB's New Trojan Horse*, to the topic. "During the Soviet period," wrote Preobrazhensky, "the Moscow Patriarchate [of the Russian Orthodox Church] bishops were all KGB agents, and the highest of them were also members of the Communist Party." The FSB is the successor to the KGB. Interestingly, however, the Russian

Orthodox world has featured some anti-New Age influences as well in the form of acceptance of the writings of Fr. Seraphim Rose (1934-1982). Russians have told me that he is considered a saint inside of Russia. His book, *Orthodoxy and the Religion of the Future*, is an excellent introduction to many of what I term "the hidden dangers" of the New Age worldview.

One popular New Age publication, *New Dawn*, runs such bizarre articles as "Nazi Flying Saucers," a topic popular with Steve Quayle, a frequent guest on the Alex Jones show, who claims there is a secret Nazi UFO base under the ice. *New Dawn* writers include Richard Smoley, the former editor of *Gnosis: A Journal of the Western Inner Traditions*, and currently editor of *Quest: Journal of the Theosophical Society in America* and of Quest Books.

While Oprah sometimes appears to avoid most of these fringe elements, she clearly helped legitimize one of the worst of the worst -- the "Sweat Lodge Guru," James Ray, whose sweat-lodge "self-help" or "Spiritual Warrior" retreats resulted in three deaths. The relative of one victim said her sister learned about Ray and decided to attend one of his retreats, after watching him on "The Oprah Winfrey Show." The intense sweat lodge, at a cost of $10,000, was preceded by fasting and was supposed to result in a "re-birthing" experience.

Some observers note that Oprah's activities have already crossed the line into dangerous quackery and hucksterism. In 2006, Winfrey endorsed a book and video called "The Secret," by New Age guru Rhonda Byrne, which promised that people could have anything they want through the power of visualization and positive thinking. The book is listed as a best-seller in the "paranormal" and "occult" section of Amazon.

During her 25-year reign as host of "The Oprah Winfrey Show," from 1986 to 2011, Oprah repeatedly showed a weakness for crackpots and quackery. She promoted the James Frey book, *A Million Little Pieces*, which turned out to be fiction described as fact. Frey eventually admitted that he had tried to get the book published as a novel and that it contained embellishments about his history of drug addiction.

Despite these setbacks, Oprah's influence is a major reason why millions of our fellow citizens are becoming open and proud members of this New Age movement. Some practice meditation or smoke dope to experience God within. Any technique that will put one in an altered state will do. One popular form of this now is called "Mindfulness." As I see it, that is "mindlessness."

Winfrey didn't have to promote this controversial New Age movement, since she had succeeded in both theatrical and media fields and didn't have to go into cultural and political change. She had become widely known to the American public as one of the lead actresses in "The Color Purple." [64]   But as she acquired more wealth she became the "chosen one" for the New Age and her influence continues and expands. She could become the power broker in the Democratic presidential nomination race in 2020.

Her Oprah magazine has become openly political, with the June 2018 issue featuring her friend Gayle King's endorsement of the HBO cable channel's pro-Obama film, "The Final Year," a sympathetic look at Obama's disastrous foreign policy.

Ominously, Oprah has gone beyond promoting the New Age to embracing revolutionary ideas and even drug use. The April 2018 edition of her "Oprah Magazine" featured such articles as "Is Marijuana the New Merlot?" and the quotation, "You cannot buy the revolution. You cannot make the revolution. You can only be the revolution. It is in your spirit, or it is nowhere."

The article about marijuana as the "New Merlot" was titled, "Welcome to 'High Tea:' Why Moms Are Getting Mellow with Cannabis-Laced Tea," and advocated mind-altering drugs for mothers. "I arrived at the tiled-roof home in an Uber since I knew I'd be spending the evening sipping hot tea infused with high-grade cannabis," declared the author. [65] In Colorado, however, a mother of two children was killed by her husband, Richard Kirk, who began hallucinating after eating a marijuana cookie. Marijuana-induced mental illness is a subject of increasing concern in the scientific and medical community.

From Christian to New Ager

Who is Oprah Winfrey? How and when did she, a girl whose formative years were spent mostly with family members with deep religious convictions, come to lose her faith in basic Christian doctrines? When and how did she come to adopt and then proselytize a New Age World view? Why has Oprah denied being a New Ager?[66]

I like to think I played a role in bringing the inner-workings of the New Age Movement to the attention of Christian churches, including the Vatican. Under Pope John Paul II, Vatican warnings were issued about the incompatibility of the New Age Movement with Christianity. A Vatican document called this a "false utopia" and warned that the New Age Movement incorporates the idea that "People's way of thinking should be completely changed and there should no longer be the ancient separation of male and female. Human beings should be systematically called to take on an androgynous form of life in which each of the two sides of the brain gets used in harmony at the right time, and they should not be disconnected as they are today."

This is precisely what transpired under the presidency of Barack Hussein Obama and helps explain his focus, even in public elementary schools, on his administration imposing a transgender ideology.

In this case, however, it appears that Oprah's magazine rushed into print with some dubious allegations against a prominent Christian organization. Her April 2018 magazine hailed a person named Silas Musick, a "gender-justice crusader" and carried the headlines, "Silas Musick is Living His Truth - and Wants to Help You Live Yours. After enduring conversion therapy, Silas Musick converted himself - into a gender-justice crusader." It stated:

> Sarah Musick spent the first 18 years of her life as the dutiful, overachieving daughter of a Southern Baptist pastor in small-town Virginia. Then she went to college and fell in love-with another woman. After graduating, she spent six intensive months at Colorado's Focus on the Family Institute , trying to pray away her "dirty thoughts" about women. It didn't work. Four years later, guilt and shame led her to try to hang herself, then swallow handfuls of pills washed down with tequila. [67]

Sarah/Silas Musick had stated in testimony at the Colorado state legislature that, after speaking with her parents, "They decided it was best to send me to Focus on the Family to seek treatment." Later, she testified, "In my early days here, I met with a gender issues analyst at Focus. I came here to be de-gayed through conversion therapy – the other term, reparative therapy, that's been used." [68] When asked about this, Jeff Johnston, issues analyst for Focus on the Family, told Cliff Kincaid:

To clarify, Focus on the Family does not offer – nor have we ever offered – "reparative therapy," "treatment," "de-gaying," "conversion therapy" or any other kind of "sexual orientation change effort." None of our issues analysts are therapists and none of us provide therapy or counseling. Ms. Musick attended our student, college-level academic institute for a semester which does not include or offer any therapy or sexuality counseling.

Publishing this attack on the well-respected group Focus on the Family suggests an ominous anti-Christian turn in Oprah's transformation, with a dangerous embrace of fraudulent and dangerous gender bender experiments on young people.

Her Childhood

Oprah was born in Kosciusko, Mississippi, where she was raised a Christian and lived her first few years with her Grandmother and an Aunt Hattie. She then joined her mother Vernita who moved north to seek employment in Milwaukee, Wisconsin. After troubles with her mother that might have resulted in her having juvenile detention in Milwaukee, Oprah was then sent to live with her Father Vernon Winfrey and stepmother Zelma in Nashville, Tennessee, for her high school years that she completed in a newly integrated school.

During her young childhood years in Kosciusko and high school (sophomore year forward) and college years with her father Vernon, Oprah was "raised in Church." She was treated well by her white classmates at East High School in Nashville, Tennessee, even enjoying election to student body Vice President.[69]

Although she has painted a picture of being raised in poverty and discrimination, the more accurate portrayal, such as conveyed in Kitty Kelley's unauthorized biography, shows that she had loving parents and grandparents, and had guidance insuring academic excellence and the forensic and media skills that would give her the confidence to succeed. She was not raised in abject poverty as she claimed. Her unmarried mother, Vernita, did the best she could with the resources and jobs she had. When she could cope no longer, she sent her to live with her father back in Nashville. He and his wife (Oprah's stepmother Zelma) willingly met their responsibilities, steering Oprah's education. Oprah attended an integrated high school and was popular enough to become Vice President of her senior class.[70]

Oprah's YouTube video productions reveal a person with deep New Age convictions. Despite that, from time to time she has claimed herself to be "Christian," while at the same time decrying those saying "Jesus is the only way," including her own family members.[71] I write this with apologies to Kitty Kelley who clearly did her homework for her unauthorized biography. Kelley recounts family member disputing allegations Oprah made about their family – including opinions that she may have made false allegations of sexual abuse against family members.[72]

Oprah's first Chicago television shows had more of a sensationalist format. But they earned her a following. Sex sells and Oprah's early shows definitely featured sensationalized sexual content. It took the form of sob-filled, even lurid confessions, joined by Oprah crying with her guests and professing her own alleged personal experiences of family-member sexual abuse. One Chicago newspaper critic reportedly carried this headline about Oprah and her early Chicago programming: "When nothing is off Limits: Oprah Winfrey Profits from Porn Stars' Appeal."[73]

Her influence stems mostly more from her television talk show which aired from 1986-2011. Oprah Winfrey had made herself "the source of big book sales" and both authors and publishers scurried to find favor with her. Oprah was influential in making wealthy authors of such openly New Age writers as Deepak Chopra, Marianne Williamson and Eckart Tolle.

Winfrey does not come from a New Age background – at least on her Father's side of the house. Both her father and a first cousin have publicly by name decried Oprah Winfrey's denial of traditional Christian doctrine and embrace of New Age ones.[74]

Oprah rightfully once proclaimed that she grew up in church and indeed that was true – both her mother's family and her father's family were devout Baptist believers. Her Aunt Katharine kept her well-read Bible by her bedside. Katharine's daughter, Jo Baldwin, Ph.D., a highly intelligent, University faculty member who also is a Baptist preacher herself publicly disclosed that she was fired by Oprah for talking about Jesus.[75] Oprah's family members publicly decried Oprah's lies and exaggerations about her claimed childhood deprivations and for her turning to Christianity.[76] Per Kitty Kelley, family member Dr. Jo Baldwin, Ph.D., recounted to her that Oprah said she would "sue her pants off" if Baldwin ever disclosed the things she had learned about Oprah. Baldwin characterized her famous cousin as "dangerous and powerful." Dr. Baldwin also discussed Oprah's hostility to her Jesus-based Christian religion, saying, "Mainly, Oprah wanted to shame me for being a follower of Jesus as if to say, 'What is He doing for you that's so great?' Oprah inflicts emotional wounds that could lead to physical illness, if they aren't healed. My faith has kept me from getting sick [over her]."[77]

Her reported rejection of family Jesus-based Christianity has received either witting or unwitting support from some dedicated Christian clergy. Still, Winfrey seems open to Christianity in some form. She was interviewed by a woman who started life named after a Biblical character in the book of Ruth (Orpah), [78] Her "SuperSoul Sunday" show on the Oprah Winfrey Network does feature some traditional Christians. It is because of the perception that Oprah is a traditional Bible-believing Christian that her political activities carry such significance.

She was a major factor in Barack Obama's 2008 Presidential election – his political career having been relatively limited and his presidential tenure the longest he ever held a job. It was Oprah Winfrey who was first reported as saying she would "like to see Barack Obama become President." That declaration by Oprah Winfrey probably was a death knell of sorts for Hillary Clinton's presidential aspirations. Her former New Age allies abandoned her campaign in favor of Obama. The obvious reason being that they didn't want to cross Oprah Winfrey, the chief popularizer of their books, seminars, and media appearances. Although Jean Houston and Marianne Williamson had enjoyed White House proximity and access during Bill Clinton's presidency, they shunned Hillary during her 2008 presidential campaign. The reason? Oprah had blessed Obama.

Oprah was equally a major force in Hillary Clinton not winning the Democratic nomination for President in 2008. Hillary Clinton had courted a crowd of New Age and self-help luminaries as Tony Robbins, Marianne Williamson, Catherine Bateson, Steve Covey, and Jean Houston. They were given both White House and Camp David access during her husband's Presidency. Hillary counted upon them for support. Instead of support, they shunned her presidential campaign and instead gave their support to a relatively late comer to national politics -- Barack Obama. The obvious reason? Again, they were not about to cross Oprah Winfrey, who was responsible, they thought, for their large volume book sales.

Despite the questions about the exercise of her power, Oprah has shaped presidential elections and could do so again in 2020.

This movement, symptomatic of a "post-Christian" America, surfaced in a big way during the 2016 Democratic presidential campaign. Cliff Kincaid covered one Sanders rally and reported that "[T]he huge crowds which greeting socialist Bernie Sanders in his run for the Democratic presidential nomination could not just be attributed to large numbers of left-wingers. There was a hard-core left-wing element to the Sanders candidacy, of course. But Sanders had tapped into what used to be one of Hillary Clinton's former key constituencies, the New Age Movement."

A top Sanders adviser turned out to be Marianne Williamson, whose self-help books were heavily promoted by Oprah Winfrey and sold millions. Oprah's website describes Williamson in particular as "a pioneer on the front lines of a worldwide spiritual movement aimed at creating a global shift in collective consciousness." Williamson, who wrote on the Sanders-for-president website about the need for "revolutionary power," has used her vast influence to mobilize her followers on behalf of the "progressive" wing of the Democratic Party. She believes the presidency of Barack Obama wasn't radical enough.

Relatively late to the New Age game, Oprah Winfrey's reported conversion started with her interview of Marilyn Ferguson on a 1987 program.[79] She went on to become an enthusiastic convert and open promoter. There may have been earlier influences. Oprah, per Kitty Kelley's biography, viewed poet Maya Angelou as a mother figure. She carried Maya Angelou's itinerary with her daily, said Oprah.[80] Maya Angelou's book, *I Know Why the Caged Bird Sings,* has been a New Age classic as long as I have been aware of the New Age Movement. It is listed as one of 250 representative New Age books in Mark Satin's New Age Politics. [81] The book by Satin, a "former" Marxist and a member of SDS, the forerunner to the Weather Underground, is described as "insights from the feminist, ecology, human-potential, spiritual, decentralist, world-order, and similar movements" integrated "into a holistic new political philosophy or ideology…"

I take personal note that this was five years after my own pioneering work against New Age principals went public nationally in 1982. I suspect Oprah's family was familiar with my work and preaching against New Age doctrines, including the teaching that there could be a Christ other than Jesus. Her father Vernon, her Aunt Katharine, and her cousin, Jo Baldwin, Ph.D., all spoke disapprovingly of Oprah's abandonment of Jesus and adoption of New Age religion. (Kelley, 2010)[82]

Another influence on Oprah was "New Thought" writer Eric Butterworth. The New Agers she went on to popularize had been "bubble gum card" personalities long before 1987. But Oprah had a platform -- a huge media platform that she would use to proselytize her new-found belief that humans, too, were divine.

Equally, if not even more disturbing than her personal adoption and popularization of New Age beliefs, is the portrayal of Oprah Winfrey's propensity for complete control of publicity, people, and projects under her. Obviously, she has shrewdly and probably accurately figured that in too many instances, people would dance for money. And money is what Oprah has. She is reportedly the first African-American woman billionaire and has a net worth of $2.8 billion.

I believe that a spiritually lethal combination of New Age beliefs combined with controlling personality tendencies have made Oprah a potentially dangerous force in religious and political life.

Black clergyman T. D. Jakes has reportedly been a factor in Oprah Winfrey's spiritual life. He was well in a position to perhaps reinforce her family's concerns about the crumbling of Oprah's Christianity in favor of New Age beliefs. Instead, wittingly or unwittingly, he reinforced her New Age belief that she was spiritually evolved far beyond her allegedly backward family. She reportedly broke down in tears during her interview of Jakes' when he told her she should meet family members "where they are." She obviously took this as confirmation of the "superiority" of her own evolved beliefs.

Oprah Winfrey believes one goes inside for "wisdom." She believes she has achieved the wealth and fame she has because she had a different personal vision for herself than the more limiting beliefs of her family, e.g., her grandma hanging clothes and having a vision for Oprah that she would also grow up to be a maid to "good white folks." Oprah said she had a bigger dream for herself.

However, neither the Old Testament prophets nor Jesus suggested one should go "inside" for wisdom. I opened my own Bible to check for myself. Consider Jeremiah 10:23:

> O Lord, I know that the way of man is not in himself : it is not in man that walketh to direct his steps.[83]   O Lord, correct me, but with judgment; not in thine anger, lest thou bring me to nothing.[84]

And if you are averse to stern Old Testament prophets, consider the words of Jesus to his disciples:

> For from within, out of the heart of men, proceed evil thoughts, adulteries, fornications, murders, thefts, covetousness, wickedness, deceit, lasciviousness, an evil eye, blasphemy, pride, foolishness . . . (Gospel of Mark, Chapter 7)

Oprah does sometimes offer valid advice on persistence and that our existence as human beings here is not an accident. However, she gives credit to "the creation" rather than to the Creator and his mediator with man, Jesus Christ.

In my view, after studying this movement for decades, I believe Oprah uses her huge platform to preach a very New Age type of gospel that comes closer to the biblical profile of "such as do wickedly against the covenant, shall he corrupt by flatteries." The flatteries of "you are God" and "you teamed up with the Force are omnipotent" are very old and effective ones. Oprah delivers them in a most hypnotic matter. And that is why her influence is both coveted and dangerous. Oprah almost single-handedly gave us President Barack Hussein Obama. How will she use her considerable financial and political clout come 2020?

What will happen if Oprah changes course or comes into public disfavor such as has happened to other media exploited personalities? As with Jim Jones and Jonestown, the New Age Movement will march on -- perhaps with the same name -- perhaps with others. They will, as they did with Jim Jones, Ira Einhorn, Marshall Applewhite, pretend that they never existed. They may even now characterize her as a "dangerous fundamentalist Christian." That is what they attempted to do with Jim Jones.

If I were Oprah, I'd now stop and reflect. As Jesus said, "what doth it profit a man if he gain the whole world, but lose his own soul?" My prayer for Oprah is that she will listen to her own concerned family members who tried to warn her of the readily apparent "New Age" dangers to her soul.

## Obama's Stake in the Homosexual Revolution

By Peter LaBarbera

> "I think that people, irrespective of their
> political views or partisan identification, will
> be…profoundly astonished about how much
> substance of Barack Obama's life has not
> previously been made known." -- David J.
> Garrow, author, *Rising Star: The Making of
> Barack Obama*

Barack Obama is easily the most pro-homosexual
president in U.S. history, becoming a "fierce
advocate" of gay rights, according to one homosexual
writer.[85] Working directly with homosexual and
transgender activist groups, he made more than 250
openly LGBTQ appointments at the federal level --
including the first openly homosexual Secretary of
the Army, Eric Fanning.[86] The scope of Obama's pro-
gay record is astonishing. So great was his devotion
to advancing homosexuality and extreme gender
confusion ("transgenderism") in the name of "civil
rights" that many observers pro and con say his
proudest achievement may have been advancing the
revolutionary LGBT (Lesbian, Gay, Bisexual,
Transgender) agenda during his two terms in the
White House.

With each passing year in the Oval Office, Obama
and his administration grew more aggressive in
promoting newfangled "rights" based on a sexual
perversion (homosexuality) and gender confusion
(transgenderism). Homosexual and transgender
activists hailed Obama as a hero, but their victories

often came at the expense of other citizens' constitutional and religious liberties, like the freedom to support natural, man-woman marriage and oppose sodomy as a sin.

The Chicago Democrat and former "community organizer" who seemingly came out of nowhere to assume the most powerful office in the world became such a force for "gay equality" (read: homosexual egalitarianism) that he famously lit up the White House in "rainbow flag" colors to celebrate the Supreme Court's 2015 imposition of national "gay marriage"—which only a few years before he had piously opposed as a candidate.[87] Obama was widely criticized when, after his successor, Donald Trump, lit up the White House blue in honor of fallen cops, it was revealed that Obama had refused an identical request by the Federal Law Enforcement Officers Association after a sniper killed five policemen in Dallas in 2016.[88]

"Love is love," tweeted Obama, applauding the radical SCOTUS *Obergefell v. Hodges* ruling, quoting the simplistic "gay" activist mantra intended to neutralize religious and moral opposition to homosexuality, grounded in thousands of years of Judeo-Christian history. Few pundits have speculated as to why Obama, a professed Christian, became so committed to advancing court-imposed same-sex "marriage" and homosexuality as "civil rights." Was candidate Obama's earlier "God's in the mix" opposition to same-sex "marriage" a con job on gullible American voters?

A more honest examination of Obama's life than the left-leaning media has been willing to provide may partly explain his deep commitment to the homosexual political and cultural agenda. Did Obama have a personal stake in propelling the LGBTQ (Lesbian, Gay, Bisexual, Transgender, Queer) revolution forward? What was the effect of the unique and bizarre circumstances of Obama's childhood -- including being abandoned by his parents, his extensive pot use as a teenager and then cocaine use in college, having a cross-dressing nanny and being "mentored" by a perverted Communist who had "strong homosexual tendencies"?[89] Was Obama ever on the "down low" (secretly practicing homosexuality) or, at some level, a "bisexual"? What is the significance of his comment to his first serious girlfriend that he "considered gayness" but chose to live a heterosexual life?

Obama's Sexual Past

Was there an element of self-interest or self-justification in Obama's radical embrace of all things LGBTQ? Or was he just being a good "progressive"? Speculating about people's sexual proclivities is fraught with difficulty, especially when done out of malice to slander the target. I can say that with some authority as a heterosexual family man with five kids who in the last 25 years has been repeatedly and falsely accused by homosexual activists of being a secret "gay" merely because I am devoted to exposing the radical homosexual agenda. Thus, any discussion of Obama's (potential) "sexual orientation" should be approached judiciously.

An array of conspiracy theories surrounds Obama, perhaps more than any other national political figure in U.S. history. The widespread traction in conservative circles of the "birther" controversy over whether Obama was truly born in the United States (Hawaii) --and hence eligible as a "natural born citizen" to be president -- has made it easier for other deception-based theories to take hold in the public's imagination. It is wrong to assume these theories are true without any serious corroborating evidence, especially when the allegations come from people who loathe Obama. It is also unwise to immediately discount any evidence brought forward that suggests Obama may have intentionally deceived the public about various aspects of his past that would have hindered his meteoric rise to national power.

On the sexual front, there is new evidence from a reputable source that Obama's sexual history was not fully vetted by the political press. For that matter, nor was the full extent of his past use of illegal drugs or his radical racial politics. Historian and Pulitzer Prize-winning author David Garrow in his 2017 biography, *Rising Star: The Making of Barack Obama,* is the first to report on a letter in which a youthful Obama writes that he "considered" living a "gay" life but opted for heterosexuality instead. Garrow also made news by reporting "that Obama was still using cocaine in his early 20s … a significant revelation. He had previously only disclosed that he used it as a teenage student," reported the UK *Daily Mail*.[90]

"I think that people, irrespective of their political views or partisan identification, will be astonished about how much substance of Barack Obama's life has not previously been made known," Garrow told podcaster Jamie Weinstein.[91]

Here is the passage from *Rising Star* on Obama and "gayness" (emphasis added):

> "[Openly homosexual Occidental College assistant professor Lawrence] Goldyn made a huge impact on Barack Obama….
>
> "Goldyn years later would remember that Obama 'was not fearful of being associated with me' in terms of 'talking socially' and 'learning from me' after as well as in class. Three years later [after studying as a freshman at OC under Goldyn] Obama wrote somewhat elusively to his first intimate girlfriend that he thought about and considered gayness, but ultimately had decided that a same-sex relationship would be less challenging and demanding than developing one with the opposite sex. But there is no doubt that Goldyn gave eighteen-year-old Barry [Soetoro, Obama's childhood name using the surname of his Indonesian stepfather] a vastly more positive and uplifting image of gay identity and self-confidence than he had known in Honolulu."[92]

In his interview with Weinstein, Garrow answers "No" to the direct question of whether Obama is "secretly gay." Weinstein asks, "Any time in his life?" Garrow again responds, "No." Weinstein then circles back to seek clarification on the same point. Note how Garrow dodges the question:

> Weinstein: I just want to go back to one question because there was a pause there [in Garrow's response] that made me want to press a little bit closer to this. Let me rephrase one of the conspiracies: was there any time in Barack Obama's life that he experimented outside of the heterosexual lifestyle?

> Garrow: I think anyone and everyone, no matter what their role in life, deserves a certain basic degree of privacy in that context. So that's not something that I speculate upon either in the book or in speaking about him. Prior to Michelle Robinson, Barack had three major serious relationships: Alex [McNear], Genevieve [Cook]... [and Sheila Jager]. But one should not look at those relationships as being more important in kind than his [intellectual] relationships [with people like Harvard Law School classmate Rob Fisher]...

> I think it's really imperative for people to focus on Barack as an intellectually serious person, and an extremely political person, from Springfield forward, from the 1990s forward. I think those are the contexts in which Barack should be understood and critiqued, and -- whether with girlfriends or whether with drug use when one's in high school or college--I think those are matters of

relatively secondary or indeed tertiary importance.[93]

In another interview with C-SPAN founder and retired CEO Brian Lamb, Garrow said that making an issue of the young Obama's potential "gayness" issue amounts to "tabloidization." Here is the excerpt (emphasis added):

> Lamb: Some journalists have picked out of your book that moment where [Obama] wrote a letter saying that he was thinking of the gay life, but explain all this and Lawrence Goldyn.

> Garrow: Lawrence Goldyn was a young Political Science professor at Occidental College. Barack was at Occidental for his first two years of college, 1979 to '81, then transferred to Columbia University in New York. And just as Barack says in that clip, and as he said years earlier in interviews with gay journalists back in 2004, 2008, Goldyn had a big impact on him. And being an openly proud and out gay person, gay professor, gay academic in 1980, people who are much younger may not fully fathom how path-breaking that was at that point in time. So there's no question that Goldyn had a significant impact on Barack, as did a number of other professors.

> Garrow: There is one passage in a letter to Alex McNear, Barack's first girlfriend, where he makes reference to his thoughts about gayness. Now, Barack's letters to Alex are I

think--verbose or prolix would not be unkind adjectives to use. Alex has never wanted the precise language printed, so I am relying on her description of that passage to me. We don't have the exact wording. This is something that I flagged and described to Barack. He was 110 percent untroubled by it. I think I can say that without violating the off-the-record thing [Garrow's off-the-record interviews with Obama]. So for a few tabloid people to try to make something of that is simply tabloidization.[94]

Garrow's editorializing aside, even in this politically correct age fueled by the media's ubiquitous pro-LGBT messaging, it is odd for a heterosexual man to say that he "considered gayness." So the new revelation in *Rising Star* implies that Obama either: 1) once practiced homosexual behavior (and still does?); 2) had the opportunity to do so (or was seduced into it); or 3) at least had enough same-sex attractions (sexual confusion issues) to consider this as a viable identity and way of life.

Yet Garrow, whose book contains ample facts about Obama's sexual relationships with Obama's girlfriends, fails to investigate this aberrant facet of Obama's past beyond reporting the latter's "gay" acquaintances. (Nor does he mention the Larry Sinclair allegations, even to shoot them down; see below.) Was the biographer protecting Obama's reputation or reluctant to delve into his potential (past) homosexuality for ideological reasons? In such a mammoth volume in which 271 pages are devoted just to the endnotes alone, why wasn't this portion of Obama's life investigated further—especially since advancing "gay rights" became perhaps Obama's proudest and most enduring legacy?

Here it deserves mentioning that Garrow is a Bernie Sanders supporter who voted for Obama, and whose writings demonstrate strong support for "gay rights" and homosexual "marriage" as a civil rights issue." [95]

Also, it is important to remember that "down low" homosexuality is precisely behavior carried on by (predominately Black) men who do not identify as "gay." Thus, had Obama ever engaged in homoerotic behavior or secret homosexual acts as an adult -- or experimented as a teen -- he could still affirm that he is not nor ever was "gay."[96]

Perverse Influences

Barack Obama (Barry Soetoro) had so many dysfunctional and perverse influences in his life growing up that it would almost be strange for him *not* to develop some sort of sexual or psychological confusion. Most prominently, his absent father and his mother abandoning him for professional pursuits for long stretches of his life surely were not healthy factors in young Barry's formative years. ("The father plays a pivotal role in a boy's normal development as a male," wrote the late Dr. Joseph Nicolosi in *A Parent's Guide to Preventing Homosexuality*. "The truth is, Dad is more important to the boy's gender-identity development than is Mom.")[97]

Here are a few other harmful -- and shocking -- influences on Obama as described in Garrow's book:

- Young Barry had a cross-dressing nanny in Jakarta. Garrow writes: "Before the spring of 1970 was out [Barry was eight years-old], and with a second child] the way, Ann [Dunham, Obama's mother] hired an openly gay twenty-four-year-old, sometimes cross-dressing man—Turdi by day, Evie by night—to be both cook and nanny….Turdi often accompanied Barry to and from school. Later, Turdi, at age sixty-six, told the Associated Press: "I never let him see me wearing women's clothes. But he did see me trying on his mother's lipstick sometimes. That used to really crack me up." (p. 65)

- The marijuana supplier of Barack's dope-smoking high school "Choom Gang" was a 29-year-old homosexual pervert who showed porn films to the teenage boys: "By the fall of his junior year, Barry was a more memorable member of another Punahou assemblage, known as the Choom Gang….But the Choom Gang didn't choom tobacco, they choomed pakalolo, the Hawaiian word for marijuana…Ray Boyer, their go-to drug dealer…was haole [white, not a native Hawaiian], but just as visibly, he was gay. "Let's just say if he was closeted, he wasn't fooling anybody," Hebs [Mark Hebing] said later. The Choom Gang called him "Gay Ray." He was twenty-nine years ole, and he lived in an abandoned bus inside a deserted warehouse in Kakaako, a then-desolate neighborhood west of Waikiki. Topo [Tom Topolinksi] remembered that the scene there "was very scary...No one in their right mind would live there." Ray also had another main interest: porn "I think he was looking to convert some people," Topo said years later. "He would bring them back to his bus and stone 'em, with porn movies on—they were heterosexual porn movies, but it was still really creepy." But Ray always had good quality pakalolo on hand, so the connection was important. "Ray freaked me out. I was afraid of the guy," Topolinksi said. "But he did befriend us, and he was our connection...there were times when he would take us to a drive-in movie...He partied with us, but there was something about him that never made me feel comfortable." (p. 92)

- Obama was evidently the closest among his "Choom Gang" friends to "Gay Ray": Garrow describes Barry Soetoro's high school yearbook "ad," which include a beer bottle and joint rolling papers, and this message: "Thanks Tut, Gramps, Choom Gang, and Ray for all the good times." Garrow writes: "Decades later, that sentence would receive far less public attention and discussion than it should have. Barry, alone of all the Choom Gang, had singled out their weird, gay, porn-showing drug dealer by name and thanked

114

him 'for all the good times.' As Tom Topo frankly acknowledged, the Choom Gang *had [emphasis author's]* spent plenty of time with Gay Ray over the previous two years, but a public -- and permanent -- thank-you to their drug connection was something that all the others, even Mark Bendix, did not go so far as to put into print." (In 1986, the 37-year-old "Gay Ray" Boyer was found bludgeoned to death by a 20-year-old male prostitute, according to Garrow.) (p. 104)

▪ Obama's mentor, Communist Frank Marshall Davis, was a promiscuous pornographer who described himself as having "homosexual tendencies" and was a pedophile. Garrow confirms that Davis, a close friend of Obama's grandfather Stan Dunham, writing under the pseudonym "Bob Greene," published a "self-proclaimed sexual autobiography, *Sex Rebel: Black, Memoirs of a Gash Gourmet.* An "introduction" to the book states that the author [Frank] may have "strong homosexual tendencies." Garrow continues: "'Bob Greene' then acknowledged that 'under certain circumstances I am bisexual' … 'Bob's' dominant preference was threesomes…'Bob,' or Frank, championed recreational sex, arguing that 'this whole concept of sex-for-reproduction-only carried with it contempt for women…'" Garrow quotes Davis writing to a female friend: "what some people call pornography (I call it erotic realism)." He reports that Davis' small cottage was nicknamed "the Jungle and that it was "a place known for both sex and dope." Garrow reports that "Stan Dunham was one of Frank's best friends during the years he lived in the Jungle"….According to a younger friend Dawna, who was like an adopted daughter to Frank: "They were really good buddies. They did a lot of adventures together that they were very proud of." Garrow writes, quoting Dawna: "As of 1970 Stan 'came a couple of times a week to visit [Frank],' and the two men particularly enjoyed crafting 'a lot of limericks that were slightly off-color, and they took great fun in those' and in other discussions of sex, which Dawna would avoid."….[O]ver the next nine or ten years, Stan brought his grandson [Barack Obama, then Barry Soetoro] with him again and again when he went to visit Frank, and as Barry got older, Stan encouraged him to talk with Davis on his own." (pp. 71-72)[98]

The Larry Sinclair Story

Larry Sinclair is a homosexual with a criminal record (felony theft and forgery charges) who claims that he used cocaine with Barack Obama twice in 1999 and performed oral sex on him both times, after meeting the then-Illinois state senator with the help of Sinclair's rented limousine driver on a visit to Chicago. Sinclair said he remembered the Obama encounter when, in 2004 and living in Mexico, he spotted the Illinois politician on TV giving the primetime Democratic National Committee speech that would catapult him to political stardom.

Subsequently, when Obama was running for the presidency in 2007, Sinclair said he repeatedly contacted the Obama campaign to request that the now-U.S. Senator correct the record about ending his drug use back in high school, to reflect the crack cocaine he allegedly smoked with Sinclair in 1999 (in the back of the limo and in Sinclair's hotel room). Sinclair stresses that he first sought to correct the record only on Obama's drug use—and did not mention the oral sex--but when his efforts to obtain a public correction were stymied he was forced to expose the homosexual encounters to provide context of what he said had transpired between the two.

After Sinclair appealed to the Obama campaign for months to correct the public record, he said he began to be contacted by a man named "Donald," who later turned out to be Donald Young, the choir director of Trinity United Church of Christ, Obama's church then pastored by the notorious Jeremiah Wright. In one phone exchange "Donald" asked him if was going to go public about the sex with Obama, even though Sinclair had not yet mentioned it to the Obama campaign, he claims.

Young was gunned to death on the day before Christmas in 2007 in his South Side Chicago home.[99] Sinclair claims that after several phone conversations, Young had intimated to him that he (Young) and Obama were homosexual lovers, despite Obama's marriage to Michelle. Sinclair claims that Young was murdered by people connected to Obama to keep him from revealing their "down low" (secret homosexual) liaisons.

Left-wing publications like *The Nation* ridiculed Sinclair's story, while some conservative outlets like WorldNetDaily (WND.com), as well as a host of right-wing bloggers, took it seriously. Former WND staff writer Jerome Corsi penned a series of WND articles building on Sinclair's allegations against Obama. One reported that Wright's church ran an informal "Down Low Club" of sorts that paired closeted homosexual men attending the church with women who would serve as a cover ("beard") to hide their homosexuality and earn them respectability in Chicago's Black community.[100]

Corsi and WND reported that Obama in his earlier Chicago days would frequent homosexual bars and a Chicago "gay" bathhouse, Man's Country[101] (which closed on New Year's Day 2018).[102]

The dominant media had no interest in such stories, which generally failed to quote people who would go on record as actually having seen Obama at a "gay" sex establishment or even a homosexual bar in the city's "gay" Boystown neighborhood.

Critics of Larry Sinclair point to his past criminal convictions[103] and say he failed to provide hard evidence backing up key aspects of his story.

The *Washington Examiner* said "Sinclair's gender does not match Obama's reported preference." Yet, Obama's presidency was characterized by relentless efforts to normalize homosexality as well as transgenderism.

Despite the questions, Sinclair's lawyer, Montgomery Blair Sibley, told Cliff Kincaid, "Yes, I believed Larry when he made his claim. I got a verbal confirmation from the chauffeur, Paramjit Multani, that night who then disappeared on me. I know we could have confirmed Obama's cell phone was at the time and location that Larry alleged the assignation occurred, but was blocked from getting that information by the Court."

Ultimately, they chose to hold a news conference at the National Press Club "as Larry was genuinely concerned with his safety given the curious death of the openly-gay choir-director of the church in Chicago of which Obama was a member for some 20 years -- Jeremiah Wright's Trinity United Church of Christ -- with whom he had traded text messages shortly before his death. He was immediately arrested on a Delaware warrant after the press event issued by Joe Biden's late son. Curious events then followed."

Many who have heard Sinclair's story say it sounds believable; he has been consistent over the years in telling it and he recounts many details that add to the authenticity of the story. Moreover, many who think Sinclair is telling the truth wonder why he would lay out his entire troubled history, including his own criminality -- and subject himself to further retribution -- for a lie. (His critics counter that his reward is the fame he has gained since coming forward.) Lastly, a critic of polygraph tests says that the results of Sinclair's test -- strangely commissioned by a porn site whose owner supported Obama -- were not interpreted correctly and that the digital results of Sinclair's test have him passing it.[104]

A factor seemingly in Sinclair's favor is that he has refused to recant his story despite being subjected to a mountain of harassment from pro-Obama forces. After coming forward, he faced all sorts of antics designed to discredit him, including, he alleges, selective criminal prosecution by those he says were desperate to silence him to protect Obama. As noted, Sinclair was arrested immediately following his Press Club event for a past criminal offense, at the behest of the Delaware Attorney General Beau Biden, the late son of eventual Obama running-mate, Sen. Joe Biden. There were also false reports on hostile web sites that Sinclair was dead and that he had retracted his story.[105]

Obama's Drug Deception

Another reason not to dismiss Sinclair's claims out-of-hand is Garrow's revelation that candidate Obama deceived the public about when he actually quit using cocaine (the drug habit continued past his college years). This was precisely the focus of Sinclair's original intent to hold Obama accountable. Sinclair said emphatically that he first sought only to get the Obama campaign to admit, in the name of its much-vaunted "transparency," that the Illinois Senator had used crack cocaine as recently as 1999, as opposed to quitting in college. Only after his appeals to the campaign were rejected, Sinclair said, did he tell the story about the homosexual sex acts he twice allegedly performed on Obama--because he knew he would be pressed for the full details surrounding the circumstances of his alleged drug use with Obama.

Nevertheless, many observers, and Sinclair himself, have questioned why Sinclair was ridiculed or ignored after confronting Obama, and not given the benefit of the doubt by the media, while women who allege sexual harassment against Republican candidates—including Herman Cain and Donald Trump -- routinely are presumed by the media to be telling the truth. Sinclair himself recently questioned why the media is taking everything Stormy Daniels says about Donald Trump seriously while it dismissed and mocked his allegations about Barack Obama.[106]

The media's double-standard on presidential sex scandals is obvious. While Sinclair's sensational allegations were never confirmed, there is no indication that most major media seriously investigated them. But with the media's "non-coverage" of Obama it went well beyond that, as biographer Garrow discovered that few reporters went back into Obama's youthful school and college days to interview school classmates who could have provided Americans with more information with which to evaluate the potential president.

Had Obama been a Republican, surely the Sinclair-type allegations would have been taken more seriously by the media. And if Garrow-type reporting had occurred when Obama was running, the nation's voters would have learned much more about his drug use, his far-left views on race, and the radical influences that helped shape his thinking, potentially tilting the election.

Obama's "Gay Marriage" Con

Regardless of his personal sexual proclivities, it would be difficult to overstate the political and cultural tidal wave of pro-LGBTQ public policies and advocacy that Barack Obama ushered in as president, particularly after he flip-flopped on homosexual "marriage." As a "progressive" in deep sympathy with LGBTQ lobby groups like Human Rights Campaign, Obama served as a "cool" catalyst for and rewarder of "gay" power --taking it to heights unimaginable just a decade ago. To be fair, his presidency came after decades of escalating "gay" activism and the media's unrelenting push for homosexual and transgender "rights"—in which moral critics of LGBT advocacy were demonized as "haters" and "homophobes" and boxed out of the public square.

No aspect of Obama's gay agenda is more important than his deceptive, politically correct "evolution" on homosexual "marriage," which has far-reaching repercussions for Americans' freedom of conscience and the well-being of our youth. Conservatives and Republican pundits like to use Obama's former opposition to "gay marriage" as a talking point, claiming it paralleled that of Republican standard-bearers like John McCain and Mitt Romney. But this is far from the truth. As a "progressive" Chicago Democrat, Obama was reflexively pro-homosexual, having grown up under the influence of leftist, atheistic family members and friends (and a perverted Communist mentor, Frank Marshall Davis). [107] He was also "radicalized" on the issue by an openly homosexual professor at Occidental College, where he attended as an undergraduate.

Note Obama's commitment to the homosexual agenda when he was running for U.S. Senate in this 2004 letter to the "gay" Chicago newspaper, *Windy City Times* --in which he labeled the bipartisan federal "Defense of Marriage Act" (DOMA) as "abhorrent." Also note how Obama imputes only sinister motives to those attempting to preserve the integrity of marriage as between a man and a woman:

Letter to Windy City Times

2004-02-11

As an African-American man, a child of an interracial marriage, a committed scholar, attorney and activist who works to protect the Bill of Rights, I am sensitive to the struggle for civil rights. As a state Senator, I have taken on the issue of civil rights for the LGBT community as if they were my own struggle because I believe strongly that the infringement of rights for any one group eventually endangers the rights enjoyed under law by the entire population. Since 1996, I have been the sponsor or a chief co-sponsor of measures to expand civil liberties for the LGBT community including hate-crimes legislation, adoption rights and the extension of basic civil rights to protect LGBT persons from discrimination in housing, public accommodations, employment and credit.

Today, I am a candidate for the U.S. Senate. Unlike any of my opponents, I have a legislative track record. No one has to guess about what I will do in Washington. My record makes it very clear. I will be an unapologetic voice for civil rights in the U.S. Senate.

For the record, I opposed DOMA [ the Defense of Marriage Act ] in 1996. It should be repealed and I will vote for its repeal on the Senate floor. I will also oppose any proposal to amend the U.S. Constitution to ban gays and lesbians from marrying. This is an effort to demonize people for political advantage, and should be resisted. ...

When Members of Congress passed DOMA, they were not interested in strengthening family values or protecting civil liberties. They were only interested in perpetuating division and affirming a wedge issue. ...

Despite my own feelings about an abhorrent law, the realities of modern politics persist. While the repeal of DOMA is essential, the unfortunate truth is that it is unlikely with Mr. Bush in the White House and Republicans in control of both chambers of Congress. ...

We must be careful to keep our eyes on the prize -- equal rights for every American. We must continue to fight for the Employment Non-Discrimination Act. We must vigorously expand hate-crime legislation and be vigilant about how these laws are enforced. We must continue to expand adoption rights to make them consistent and seamless throughout all 50 states, and we must repeal the 'Don't Ask, Don't Tell' military policy.

I know how important the issue of equal rights is to the LGBT community. I share your sense of urgency. If I am elected U.S. Senator, you can be confident that my colleagues in the Senate and the President will know my position.

Barack Obama

Democratic Candidate for the U.S. Senate[108]

Flip-Flop-Flip

A little-known fact is that Obama was on record as being "for" homosexuality-based "marriage" before he was "against" it (in his runs for U.S. Senate and then the presidency), before ultimately coming out for it again in 2012, to great media fanfare. Obama's media-enabled charade on "gay marriage" became clear in 2009, when the Chicago LGBT newspaper *Windy City Times* dug up an old candidate questionnaire from 1996 in which he had professed support for legalizing homosexual "marriage" (Obama was running for State Senate).[109]

But by 2004, with Obama was running for his first statewide office -- U.S. Senator from Illinois -- he was telling the *Windy City Times* that it wasn't yet practical to push for "gay marriage," so he came out for "civil unions" instead. Here is a portion of his response to a Feb. 2004 *Windy City Times* interview question on same-sex marriage (for Illinois but implicitly for the nation as well):

> WCT Editor Tracy Baim: But you think, strategically, gay marriage isn't going to happen so you won't support it at this time?
>
> Obama: What I'm saying is that strategically, I think we can get civil unions passed. I think we can get SB 101 [an Illinois LGBT "nondiscrimination" bill] passed. I think that to the extent that we can get the rights, I'm less concerned about the name ["marriage"]. And I think this is my No. 1 priority, it is an environment in which the Republicans are going to use a particular language that has all sorts of connotations to the broader culture as a wedge issue, to prevent us from moving forward, in securing those rights, then I don't want to play their game.

In her book, *Obama and the Gays: A Political Marriage,* Baim paints an even clearer picture of Obama's cynical and calculating approach to his public homosexual "marriage" stance:

> At one point, Obama asked for the tape recorder to be turned off so we could have an off-the-record conversation about same-sex

marriage. Mainly, the unrecorded portion of our discussion was about what is practical and attainable vs. what is fair in an ideal world. My emphasis to him was about how he looked on this issue in particular; I told him that because he is the product of interracial marriage, in my opinion many gays expected him—fairly or unfairly—to be more sympathetic to marriage diversity [homosexual "marriage"]. For Obama, it was all about being realistic and pragmatic. He did not say that his position was based on his religious views, a deflection he later used when stating his opposition to same-sex marriage. The religious defense began to be invoked in the general election for U.S. Senate and especially during his presidential run.[110]

Barack Finds Religion

As Obama eyed the presidency, and with state after state passing traditional marriage-protection amendments in the wake of the Massachusetts supreme judicial court's imposition of "gay marriage' on the Bay State in 2004, he adopted a symbolically conservative stance on marriage with a veneer of religious piety to sway the masses. In an April 2008 debate against Republican Senator John McCain at Pastor Rick Warren's Saddleback Church in Lake Forest, California, Obama answered as follows in response to a question about marriage:

> I believe that marriage is the union between a man and a woman. Now, for me as a Christian

-- for me -- for me as a Christian, it is also a sacred union. God's in the mix.[111]

Journalists often reported that Obama's position on homosexual "marriage" was identical to McCain's, even though the latter was far more conservative on social issues and adhered to most of the GOP's pro-family platform against "gay rights."

In contrast, Obama's much-vaunted opposition to homosexual "marriage" was largely symbolic. He favored a federal "civil unions" law for homosexuals that essentially was "gay marriage" minus the name—telling the powerful LGBT lobby group Human Rights Campaign, "I believe civil unions should include the same legal rights that accompany a marriage license."[112] Obama pledged to sign a pro-LGBT "hate crimes" bill and end the military's "Don't Ask, Don't Tell" policy barring open homosexuality in the Armed Forces. And most importantly, he opposed federal and state "defense of marriage" amendments to preserve the ancient, natural definition of marriage as one man, one woman.

Obama's convoluted marriage positions were working at cross-purposes with each other. He was in the untenable position of, on the one hand, pledging to support traditional (one man/one woman) marriage as "sacred" while, on the other, rejecting any legislative or constitutional remedies to protect it against a high-powered LGBTQ lobby campaign to radically redefine it. But the Illinois Democrat had no reason to worry: McCain barely challenged him on social issues and most secular-liberal reporters and editors cynically viewed efforts to stop same-sex "marriage" as a GOP "wedge issue" and rarely challenged Obama to explain his contradictory positions.

Obama's War on DOMA

Once in office, Obama kept his word. After a slow start, he bended to pressure his LGBTQ allies to go all-out for "gay marriage." He set about to reverse what many of those same activists regarded as Bill Clinton's biggest "sin" -- signing the federal 1996 Defense of Marriage Act (DOMA) into law. DOMA defined marriage for federal purposes as the union of a man and a woman, and preserved states' rights not to be forced to recognize legalized same-sex "marriages" performed in other states like Massachusetts.

Obama's Department of Justice, led by far-left Attorney General Eric Holder, announced February 24, 2011 that it would no longer defend DOMA in court,[113] creating a huge advantage for LGBTQ lawyers waging a national legal campaign to eviscerate pro-traditional marriage amendments passed by voters in more than 30 states—most in electoral landslides.[114]

Beginning in the second half of his first term, it was reported that Obama's position on same-sex "marriage' was "evolving." Then, after Obama's VP, Joe Biden, forced the issue by publicly embracing "gay marriage," Obama declared his own support for it in a May 2012 TV interview with ABC's Robin

Roberts, a lesbian. He claimed that his views had "evolved," but in reality, Obama was finally coming clean on where his true sympathies had been for more than a decade. If God had been "in the mix" during Obama's first run for the presidency—when polls showed public opposition to homosexual "marriage" was well over 50 percent--the Creator of the universe was suddenly *not* in the mix as Obama tacked leftward in a culture saturated with pro-LGBTQ propaganda.

As it turned out, three years later, Obama's former top advisor, David Axelrod, would confirm that his boss only feigned opposition to same-sex "marriage" for political expediency. Wrote Axelrod in his autobiography: Obama "knew his [pro-gay-'marriage'] view was way out in front of the public's" but he "grudgingly accepted the counsel of more pragmatic folks like me, and modified his position to support civil unions rather than marriage, which he would term a 'sacred union.'"

Explaining Obama's struggles on the issue, Axelrod recalls a conversation in which the president said, "I'm just not that good at [bulls—tting]."[115] This revelation was too much even for some in the jaded, LGBT-cheerleading national media, as several news outlets reported that Obama had consciously "misled" voters on the "gay marriage" issue.[116]

Obama's Dumbed-Down "Christianity"

Another essential part of understanding Obama's escalating devotion to the homosexual-bisexual-transgender agenda was his politicized "Christianity," in which biblical proscriptions against sodomy were ignored so that this particular "social justice" cause of the Left could be enshrined. While most media parlayed the line that Obama was a "Christian," implying some fealty to biblical mores, Obama's record shows that the Bible would never stand in the way of LGBTQ "progress."

Perhaps this is understandable, as Obama was raised and mentored in part by atheists and humanists, including his mother -- described by one reporter as an "atheist, with a spiritual and humanist bent[117]-- grandparents and Communist pervert Frank Marshall Davis.

Robert Gagnon[118], the world's preeminent conservative theological expert on the Bible and homosexuality, took issue with Obama's casual dismissal of a key New Testament passage that proscribes homosexual acts as unnatural and sinful. The text in question is in the New Testament Book of Romans, Chapter 1, verses 26-27:

> Because of this, God gave them over to shameful lusts. Even their women exchanged natural relations for unnatural ones. In the same way the men also abandoned natural relations with women and were inflamed with lust for one another. Men committed indecent acts with other men, and received in themselves the due penalty for their perversion.

This passage and the verses surrounding it have been cited by many millions of Christians worldwide for millennia to show God's opposition to homosexual acts, both between men and between women. But in his book *Audacity of Hope*, Obama writes that he is not "willing to accept a reading of the Bible that considers an obscure line in Romans [about homosexual practice] to be more defining of Christianity than the Sermon on the Mount."[119]

According to Gagnon, Obama "repeated this line in a campaign appearance in Ohio … He stated that if people find controversial his views on granting the full benefits of marriage to homosexual unions, minus only the name, 'then I would just refer them to the Sermon on the Mount, which I think is, in my mind, for my faith, more central than an obscure passage in Romans.' These remarks by Obama represent a gross distortion of the witness of the Judeo-Christian Scriptures."

Writes Gagnon:

> Obama's image of Jesus is that of a person who, rather than lovingly calling sinners to repentance so that they might be reclaimed for the kingdom of God that he proclaimed, tells others to stop judging them. This is not the picture of Jesus' mission to "sinners and tax collectors" in the Gospels. Instead, we find a picture of a Jesus who aggressively reaches out in love to the biggest violators of his ethical demands while simultaneously maintaining that demand; a Jesus who encourages offenders to "go and no longer be sinning" lest something worse happen to

them, namely, exclusion from the kingdom of God. Obama does not love more or better than Jesus. That would be carrying a messianic complex a bit too far.[120]

Since Obama rejected the counsel and authority of Scripture on homosexuality, it became easier for him to support LGBTQ policy goals that, in effect, placed the achievement of "gay equality" [read: radical egalitarianism] as a "social justice" goal above the liberty and conscience rights of Christians to disagree with same-sex conduct and not participate with their small businesses in homosexuality-based "marriage."

It is telling that while many black preachers condemned Obama for so famously coming out in support of homosexuality-based "marriage," the leader of his former church, Trinity United Church of Christ, defended Obama, using the language of the social justice movement:

> Rev. Otis Moss III, who succeeded controversial Trinity lead pastor Jeremiah Wright, said, "The institution of marriage is not under attack as a result of the President's words. Marriage was under attack years ago by men who viewed women as property and children as trophies of sexual prowess," he said, drawing applause from the audience. "Marriage is under attack by low wages, high incarceration, unfair tax policy, unemployment, and lack of education."[121]

Obama Attacks Traditional Morality

President Obama's decision to direct his Attorney General Eric Holder *not* to defend DOMA, the Defense of Marriage Act that protected states from being forced to recognize "gay marriages" in other states, was a watershed moment for the social Left and a gigantic White House gift to the LGBTQ Lobby. It was also a tremendous defeat for the rule of law in America, as DOMA had been passed with bipartisan support and signed into law by a Democrat, Bill Clinton (who has since said it was a mistake).

Obama's enthusiastic and, critics said, unconstitutional use of presidential power to redefine traditional marriage played a pivotal role in undermining public support for preserving the bedrock institution. After he reneged on his 2008 campaign stance against "gay marriage," statewide votes on the issue turned in favor of "gay" activists for the first time, as pro-family advocates lost ballot campaigns to preserve the natural definition of marriage in Maryland, Maine and Minnesota.[122]

Currently the pro-family forces seeking to restore the law to defending the natural definition of marriage are in disarray, with annual pro-traditional marriage rallies drawing mere dozens of people—compared to annual pro-life marches that draw hundreds of thousands of enthusiastic defenders of the unborn. Republicans, led by resurgent, morality-averse libertarians, are moving toward embracing LGBTQ policy goals, in a tactical move to woo millennials and other younger voters.

The ease with which the "evolved" Obama began using the "gay" shibboleths and slogans of the homosexual "marriage" movement -- phrases like "love is love" and "marriage equality" -- exposed his supposed "conversion" as fraudulent. People with religious objections toward something as serious as redefining the "sacred union" of marriage as it has stood for centuries do not suddenly start parroting slogans designed to trivialize all religious and moral concerns. Also, Obama's "evolution" ultimately helped to destroy his previous promise to respect the will of millions of Americans who voted in their respective states to preserve the age-old meaning of marriage. LGBTQ activists have shown precious little "respect" for those who disagree morally with homosexuality—as increasingly they seek not only to ban them from the public square but use the law to punish those who will not bend from their principled believe that marriage can only be *sacred* as a union between a man and a woman.[123]

Now the SCOTUS *Obergefell* ruling is being used as a legal sledgehammer to force people of faith to either submit to the new LGBTQ paradigm (thereby violating their faith) or be forced out of business. In California and across the land, emboldened LGBTQ activists --with little accountability from the media -- are pushing to effectively "criminalize Christianity" by banning pro-heterosexual talk therapy that has helped men and women overcome unwanted same-sex desires. (Obama in 2015 came out against so-called "conversion therapy" ("reparative therapy") efforts designed to help youth overcome unwanted homosexual attractions and gender-confusion (transgenderism).[124]

But it must be understood that Obama was already cooperating intensely with the LGBTQ lobby in the legal campaign for the radical transformation of "marriage" long before he made the formal switch of embracing it *by name*. In that sense, Obama's pseudo-opposition to same-sex marriage and his *faux*-religious "defense" of traditional marriage were a part of a carefully orchestrated sham. Once in office, by legally crippling the defense of marriage as a "sacred union," he expedited its demise in the courts. Obama's sleight of hand on marriage -- and the rest of the radical LGBTQ agenda he pushed through as president -- were enabled by the media's sycophantic coverage of his campaign and presidency, and the GOP's failure to boldly challenge his contradictory stances.

His corrosive effect on marriage and sexual morality, and corruption of Christianity, which recognizes that it is the role of true religion to inform and defend both --free from oppression by the State -- is perhaps Barack Obama's most ominous and lasting legacy. And it was all too easy for him to accomplish, given how the dominant media rolled over and so blatantly abandoned its duty to hold accountable this mysterious, leftist candidate with a very troubling and still largely unknown background. Instead they chose to champion Obama's rise to power, and thus played a role in the calculated deceptions he carried out against the American people to win the White House.

Barack Obama's administration, seen in its totality, was fanatically devoted to the LGBTQ cause. The Alliance Defending Freedom put together a list of dozens of Obama's LGBTQ agenda items, culled from a list of President Obama's policies and statements in support of the homosexual and transgender activism. [125] The list makes it clear that Obama and his team made ample use of the White House bully pulpit to advocate for homosexuality and transgenderism.

**Obama's Reefer Madness**

By Dr. Tina Trent

When Barack Obama was elected president in 2008, drug legalization activists celebrated. Surely, the activists reasoned, this self-admitted, prolific high school "Choom Gang" pot smoker and cocaine imbiber would vocally support legalization of marijuana, at least when he reached his second term and did not need to answer to voters again.

This hoped-for relationship didn't work out as the pot activists envisioned it. Many are still seething over what they see as Obama's eight years of inaction and even obstructionism on marijuana legalization. Especially enraging to the pot lobby was the August, 2016 refusal by the Drug Enforcement Agency to reclassify marijuana from a Schedule I drug to the more lenient Schedule II "drug with accepted medical uses" under the Controlled Substances Act.

Such complaints are overstated. It is true that Obama never used his bully pulpit to proselytize for legal weed. He left the advocacy to activists in the states, where legalization efforts were advancing quickly. His inaction may also be seen as a smart political calculation: in keeping his distance, Obama may in fact have aided state-based legalization efforts by avoiding the bad optics and political fallout that would result from a president endorsing drug use from the Oval Office.

Behind the scenes, Obama's Department of Justice (DOJ) pushed Colorado, Washington, Oregon, and especially California to confront a welter of legal and regulatory issues as they built out massive new legal marijuana industries in the midst of illegal narcotics markets. This guidance by the Justice Department was crucial, even when it was resented. If California could not reign in the illegal drug cartels trying to take over the lucrative medical marijuana market, for example, or if Colorado failed to collect the windfall of marijuana taxes promised to voters, the result might be a backlash that would stall drug legalization efforts elsewhere.

As a seasoned community organizer, Obama seemed to intuit that he could be most effective by managing the expectations of the drug legalization lobby while projecting reassuring images of an orderly legalization process to the rest of the country. Community organizing isn't just about, or even primarily about staging protests: it defines permanent success in creating bureaucracies. So, rather than taking up drug legalization as an abstract civil rights issue to be fought and won at the federal level, as the activists wished, Obama focused his executive powers on the bureaucratic and regulatory side of the drug legalization movement unfolding in the states. It should surprise nobody that he helped organize this community to get what it needed, even if the drug legalizers wanted something very different from him.

In 2009, 2011, 2013, and 2014, the Obama Justice Department issued memos signaling a gradual withdrawal of enforcement of federal marijuana laws in states that had legalized the drug – with the caveat that the feds still possessed the authority to target illegal or even state-approved sales and use when they deemed such enforcement to be necessary.

The first of these memos, the 2009 Ogden Memo, sent the message that the federal government would finally offer a degree of legitimacy to the state medical marijuana industry that had existed in California since 1996. The memo stated that federal prosecutors would not:

> focus federal resources … on individuals whose actions are in clear and unambiguous compliance with existing state laws providing for the medical use of marijuana. For example, prosecution of individuals with cancer or other serious illnesses who use marijuana as part of a recommended treatment regimen consistent with applicable state law, or those caregivers in clear and unambiguous compliance with existing state law who provide such individuals with marijuana, is unlikely to be an efficient use of limited federal resources.[126]

By announcing that federal prosecutors would no longer enforce federal marijuana laws against medical marijuana users, the Odgen memo created a boomtown of marijuana production in California, Montana and Washington. Complaints about ever-expanding proliferations of "medical marijuana dispensaries" and political backlash followed, especially in California. Even some established, small-scale medical marijuana growers complained.

In response to this backlash, 2011 brought the first of three memos drafted by U.S. Deputy Attorney General James Cole. The 2011 memo was a rebuke to California for failing to rein in wholesale marijuana production and neglecting to enforce state restrictions that were supposed to govern the distribution of medical marijuana. The memo threatened a crackdown by the Department of Justice on "large-scale, privately-owned, industrial marijuana centers" and reminded state authorities that the federal position remained one of prohibition: "Congress has determined," the memo stated, "that marijuana is a dangerous drug and that the illegal distribution and sale of marijuana is a serious crime that provides a significant source of revenue to large scale criminal enterprises, gangs, and cartels."[127]

At the time, medical marijuana was already a $1.5 billion industry in California, though purportedly non-profit. The Justice Department's memorandum was accompanied by federal raids of select California pot businesses described by California's U.S. Attorneys as "hijacked by profiteers." In response to the outcry by pot legalization activists, the Justice Department declared that there was a need to pressure the state to regulate its out-of-control marijuana growers.

In contrast, and to prove the point that the federal government was not opposed to orderly de-criminalization of marijuana, Cole's 2013 memo on newly-legal recreational marijuana in Colorado and Washington sent a different message: the federal government would not use its laws to prosecute recreational users in those states. The federal government, the memo noted, "has traditionally relied on state and local law enforcement agencies to address marijuana activity through enforcement of their own narcotics laws," and they would continue to do so in those states by not prosecuting low-level recreational drug users.

In 2014, a final Cole memo tentatively committed to selectively suspending federal money laundering statutes to encouraged banks and other financial institutions to accept licensed, legal marijuana businesses as customers. The goal was to move the marijuana industry away from the dangerous, cash-only practices previously necessitated by banks' unwillingness to accept them as customers because of federal banking laws.

Obama's Long Game

Despite the federal police crackdowns after the 2011 memo, the overall effect of the Odgen and Cole memos was a dramatic liberalizing of U.S. drug law, accomplished without any oversight by Congress. As Obama entered the last two years of his presidency, there was still widespread grumbling about the 2011 Cole memo, the federal drug raids, and his failure to endorse the marijuana legalization movement. But major players who understood the long game of legalizing drugs stepped up to rehabilitate Obama's image – and, presumably, to remind their troops that democrat victories were good overall for drug legalization.

In 2014, with three out of four Americans supporting legalizing marijuana for medical uses and a majority – 51% -- supporting full legalization, *Rolling Stone* editor Jann S. Wenner and Drug Policy Alliance founder Ethan Nadelmann praised Obama for "telling the truth" about marijuana when he said in a *New Yorker* interview, "I don't think it is more dangerous than alcohol." In a prominent editorial, they urged their audience to see even the president's tepid endorsement of marijuana legalization as a "breakthrough":

> Without fanfare, Obama had just flouted decades of anti-pot propaganda by the federal government … Obama's honest assessment of the safety of marijuana and the harm of criminalizing pot users marks a seismic shift in the War on Drugs.[128]

This was crucial approval from two of the most important figures in legalization circles. It was a reminder to the grassroots that, despite the federal raids on marijuana growers in California, Obama also assisted their cause every time he took the stage to delegitimize law enforcement by branding it racist. "Obama followed his Drug War apostasy by linking the prohibition of marijuana to the racist enforcement of the nation's drug laws," Wenner and Nadelmann wrote.

However, the drug legalization movement would never get a full-throated endorsement of the virtues of marijuana from Obama. In all of his public statements on the subject, he has carefully distanced himself from the movement's reverential attitude towards marijuana and other drugs. In the 2014 *New Yorker* article cited by Wenner and Nadelmann, Obama told David Remnick:

> As has been well documented, I smoked pot as a kid, and I view it as a bad habit and a vice, not very different from the cigarettes that I smoked as a young person up through a big chunk of my adult life ... It's not something I encourage, and I've told my daughters I think it's a bad idea, a waste of time, not very healthy.[129]

Obama supported marijuana decriminalization despite this, he said, only because of the purported injustice built into the enforcement of drug laws. "It's important for society not to have a situation in which a large portion of people have at one time or another broken the law and only a select few get punished," he said. As marijuana legalization gained even more public favor in the last two years of his presidency, Obama staked out the position that marijuana should be legalized for the sole purpose of serving the greater interest of racial equality. "Middle-class kids don't get locked up for smoking pot, and poor kids do," he said repeatedly.[130]

Throughout his presidency, Obama spoke frequently of "evolving" towards better positions on topics such as gay marriage and marijuana. But he and Attorney General Eric Holder also rarely missed an opportunity to put daylight between themselves and the largely white, prosperous, "hippy-dippy" drug legalization movement. "[T]hose who argue that legalizing marijuana is a panacea and it solves all these social problems," said Obama, "I think are probably overstating the case."

The president was a true believer in other myths about drugs having to do with incarceration and crime. He claimed repeatedly that large percentages of prisoners were serving hard time for only low-level drug crimes and that prejudiced law enforcement and racial disparities in sentencing were the only meaningful factors driving the higher incarceration rates experienced by black men.

Such claims have been debunked repeatedly by careful researchers, such as Heather Mac Donald on the right and John F. Pfaff on the left. Pfaff and Mac Donald point out that it is high rates of committing violent and property crime, not drug use, that are the real drivers of high incarceration rates in the states. And even in the federal system, violent crime, trafficking and gang wars, not drug possession, are the real causes for the rise in the federal prison population.

Nevertheless, throughout his presidency, Obama rarely wasted a chance to smear law enforcement as racist and racially selective. This demonization of police was his real contribution to the drug legalization movement, and it was a valuable one.

Criminal Justice "Reform"

In 2014, Obama announced that over the last two years of his presidency, he would use his clemency powers to release thousands of prisoners who, according to him, had only committed minor crimes but were serving long federal sentences due to the mandatory minimum drug laws of the 1980's and 1990's. A year later, despite extraordinary legal resources and efforts, Obama's clemency program failed to identify a substantial percentage of prisoners who qualified even under the clemency program's broad definition of minor offenses, which read: "[i]nmates had to have served at least 10 years; [have] no significant criminal history; no connection to gangs, cartels or organized crime; and probably would have received a "substantially lower sentence" if convicted today."[131]

Desperate for better results, Obama brought in Deputy Attorney General Sally Yates to oversee the massive clemency drive. Ultimately, 4,000 attorneys from 570 law firms and 30 law schools served pro-bono to compile 16,000 clemency appeals from among the 44,000 federal inmates who applied. But by December 2016, only 1,176 inmates had been released, not all for reasons relating to drug convictions. Obama commuted the sentences of another 330 prisoners as he was leaving office. Others had their sentences shortened but remained in prison.

Despite positive media coverage, as a measure of opposing the "war on drugs," the clemency program was a disaster. Why had only some 1400 of 44,000 federal prisoners requesting clemency qualified for release? The Justice Department would not say. Nor would they offer information to confirm that all or even most of those released actually had no "significant criminal history" or involvement with gangs or international cartels. Mac Donald quickly identified more than 150 "hits" for the term "firearm" in the published commutation database, suggesting that many of those released were in fact hardened offenders with "significant criminal history."[132]

Obama's failed clemency program exposed as a lie the claim that the "war on drugs" had filled federal prisons with non-violent drug offenders serving draconian sentences for minor crimes. Federal prisons hold only 13% of all prisoners; half are in for drug trafficking charges, and virtually none are convicted for mere drug possession: "Less than 1% of sentenced drug offenders in federal court in 2014 were convicted for simple drug possession," writes Mac Donald, "and most of those convictions were plea-bargained down from trafficking charges."[133] Meanwhile, the vast majority of state prisoners, who represent 87% of all inmates, are serving time for violent felonies or property crimes. Only 16% of state prisoners are incarcerated for drug crimes, 12% for trafficking and 4% for possession, with an unknown number of those sentences resulting from plea-bargains for more serious crimes.

Even as he relentlessly demonized law enforcement, and despite his youthful drug imbibing, Obama's involvement in the modern drug legalization movement was conducted mostly from the sidelines. Still, he took credit for the progress made by others. On the morning after the surprise defeat of Hillary Clinton by Donald Trump, he made time to meet with

*Rolling Stone* editor Jann Wenner. Obama told Wenner:

> [T]his is a debate that is now ripe, much in the same way that we ended up making progress on same-sex marriage. There's something to this whole states-being-laboratories-of-democracy and an evolutionary approach. You now have about a fifth of the country where this is legal.[134]

There is little question that the country lurched towards full legalization of marijuana during the Obama years. When Obama won the presidency in 2008, recreational marijuana was not legal anywhere in the United States. Medical marijuana was legal in only thirteen states: California, Alaska, Oregon, Washington, Maine, Colorado, Hawaii, Nevada, Montana, Vermont, Rhode Island, New Mexico and Michigan. The timeline for legalization of medical marijuana in those states spanned twelve years, from 1996 to 2008.

Eight years later, when Obama walked out of the White House, sixteen more states had legalized medical marijuana, bringing the total to 29 states. Of even greater consequence, during the four years of Obama's second term in office, nine states and Washington DC legalized recreational marijuana: Colorado, Washington, Alaska, Oregon, California, Maine, Massachusetts, Nevada, Vermont, and Washington DC. With legalization came normalization in attitudes towards recreational drug taking. According to Gallup polling, in 2009, 44% of

Americans supported legalizing marijuana. In 2018, 64% do, including 51% of Republicans.

We are living through an era of actual reefer madness, so much so that it is becoming politically incorrect to express even mild negativity towards the drug, no matter who is using it. Much of this attitudinal change is the consequences of a calculated rebranding of the reputation of the drug, from a recreational substance to a "medicine" with near-magical powers of healing. So effective is this strategy that recent lifestyle articles in the *New York Times* even broach the subject of marijuana use among two groups that previously would not be considered good publicity material for legalization: pregnant women and athletes.

In "Turning to Marijuana for a Runner's High, and More," ultra-marathoner Avery Collins touts the purported benefits of the drug for his race training: "[I]t allowed me to be very present and not to worry as much about overall times and what's going on with the run," Collins says. The *Times* does quote one medical researcher who dismisses the usefulness of marijuana in sports and questions its cardiac safety, but two other researchers discuss the hypothetical benefits of marijuana or cannabidiols (non-psychoactive extracts) in achieving performance goals or treating post-exercise inflammation. One researcher complains, "[t]here hasn't been a whole lot of funding for this," but such lack of evidence is hardly slowing claims that marijuana can aide athletes' performances.[135]

Even stranger, in "A Balm When You're Expecting: Sometimes Pot Does the Trick," hundreds of *New York Times* readers responded to a query about using marijuana while pregnant. Reportedly, "most had smoked, while a few vaped or ate marijuana-laced edibles. Roughly half said they had used pot for a medical reason. Most felt marijuana use had not affected their children, or were not sure; just a handful worried the children might have suffered cognitive deficits." The *Times* story also profiles five women who used marijuana during their pregnancies, all but one of whom claim to have needed it for medical reasons, though none of the four told their doctors they were using this "medicine" to treat their pregnancies.[136]   Another *Times* story on marijuana use during pregnancy puts the number of pregnant users aged 18 to 25 at 7.5% of all pregnant women that age.[137]   Even the *Times* admits that public health research is not keeping up with the potential negative public health consequences of marijuana legalization on pregnant women and others.

Such caution is currently rare.  With marijuana being defined by non-scientist legislators and activists as both an intoxicant and a "medicine" and packaged to be eaten or rubbed on the skin as well as smoked, the legalization process itself seems optimized to encourage nonstop consumption.   And relentless lobbying for marijuana's purported virtues during the legalization battles in the states is helping fuel a veritable lifestyle revolution built around marijuana consumption.   Advocates promote the drug with quasi-religious fervor as a miracle pain medicine, a cure for opiate addiction, a tax revenue supercharger, a spirituality enhancer, and even a cancer cure.

In California, where recreational use of the drug became legal in January, there are now marijuana bake sales, marijuana mom's groups, pot-friendly co-working spaces for consuming drugs during the workday, and even marijuana snacks for cats and dogs.

As a consequence of all this hype, children and adolescents in California and other states are suddenly growing up in communities saturated with positive messages about consuming marijuana. Simultaneously, marijuana is being bred to produce stronger strains, as it was in the Netherlands after legalization there. "If you are selling an addictive product, you want as potent and addictive a product as possible," said Keith Humphreys, a professor of psychiatry and behavioral medicine at Stanford School of Medicine, "I suspect any new industry will set that as its goal."[138]

"Hef" and the Dopers

The modern marijuana legalization movement got its start in 1971, when pornographer Hugh Hefner gave $5,000 to the founders of NORML, the National Organization for the Reform of Marijuana Laws. He also gave the organization free advertising in *Playboy* magazine to solicit donations from the public. When this public campaign raised only $6,000, Hefner stepped in and pledged $100,000 a year to keep the group going.[139] In 2008, approaching its fourth decade, NORML raised $498,281 from donors.

Hefner established a pattern that would be repeated by other drug-legalization organizations: despite the seeming grassroots nature of the movement, the five major non-profits advocating for the legalization of drugs get most of their funding from a small group of extremely wealthy men. The Marijuana Policy Project (MPP) does boast 40,000 dues-paying members, but dues are only a small part of their annual fundraising: large donations are the rule. Peter Lewis, one of the original triumvirate of drug legalization billionaires that included George Soros and John Sperling, gave $3 million to MPP in 2007 alone.

From the early 1970's until the mid-1980's NORML pushed a simple legalization message: all adults should have the right to use marijuana. After this civil libertarian argument failed to advance the cause, other, more sophisticated, purportedly science-based drug legalization non-profits were launched. In 1986, Rick Doblin, a psychedelics advocate who later earned a degree from the Kennedy School of Government, started MAPS, the Multidisciplinary Association for Psychedelic Studies. In 1987, American University professor Arnold Trebach and NORML attorney Kevin B. Zeese founded the Drug Policy Foundation. In 1994, Princeton University Professor Ethan Nadelmann founded The Lindesmith Center, which has the distinction of being "the first domestic project of George Soros' Open Society Foundations."[140] Former staffers of NORML started MPP in 1995. The Lindesmith Center and the Drug Policy Foundation merged in 2000 to become the Soros-funded powerhouse, Drug Policy Alliance.

Since the infrastructure of the new legalization movement was set in place, drug legalization money from the "triumvirate of billionaires" and other wealthy donors has only increased. In 2008, when Obama was elected, the Drug Policy Alliance raised $12,489,134. In 2012, the year of Obama's re-election, their donations soared to an astonishing $47,135,352. The Marijuana Policy Project received $2,517,233 in 2008 and $3,533,657 in 2012. MAPS, which advocates for legalizing both psychedelic drugs and marijuana as "medicine," raised $2,413,863 in 2008 and $7,071,319 in 2012. According to the *Washington Times*, between 1994 and 2014, Soros alone spent $80 million through various non-profits to legalize drugs in America.[141]

In 1996, with money pouring in from the billionaires, the drug legalization movement gained its first statewide victory with the passage of Proposition 215, which made it legal to sell "medical marijuana" to people with doctors' prescriptions in California. "If those three billionaires hadn't plunked down the money," said NORML's Allen St. Pierre, "we wouldn't be talking about this right now."[142]

It is no accident that the new drug legalization movement is a movement run by academicians. Redefining marijuana as a medicine, not a recreational drug, was a strategy that harkened back to the LSD research conducted in universities in the early 1960's, when psychedelics, which were not yet street drugs, were viewed as a promising tool for enhancing psychiatric therapy and even increasing intelligence, empathy, religious insight, and human consciousness itself.

After rogue professors like Timothy Leary set out to "turn on" as many people as possible outside academic settings and helped speed the mass importation of hard drugs into mainstream American life, most universities stepped away from conducting psychedelic research. But the medical model of drug legalization was not abandoned: it moved into private foundations and alternative or "spiritual" healing centers, where psychedelic researchers like Andrew Weil and Ram Dass (Richard Alpert) continued to popularize the notion that western medical science could not perform the miracles available to people through shamanistic rituals involving psychedelics, eastern religious practices, and other alternative medicine.

George Soros saw several opportunities in California in 1996 to mount a statewide campaign to legalize marijuana there: the AIDS epidemic had given rise to a sophisticated and politically-connected activist cohort demanding access to the drug to treat wasting disease; AIDS activists, in turn, were teaching other patient groups such as cancer patients to practice confrontational politics; alternative medicine advocates like Andrew Weil were enjoying great popularity, and the old-school marijuana legalization movement was still alive in characters like Jack Herer and Steve DeAngelo.

During the campaign over Proposition 215, voters were promised that access to the drug would be limited to so-called "compassionate medical use" by people battling severe diseases such as cancer and AIDS. Voters were also assured that the amount of legal marijuana circulating in the state would be strictly limited: only "defined caregivers" serving individual patients would be permitted to grow and distribute the drug.

Both promises were deliberate falsehoods. The public face of Prop 215 was Dennis Peron, a prominent AIDS activist who helped draft the state ordinance and an earlier one that legalized marijuana for medical use in San Francisco. Television advertisements for the ballot initiative featured breast cancer sufferers and medical doctors talking about terminal pain. But behind the AIDS activists and cancer patients, George Soros alone spent more than half a million dollars directly on Prop 215.

Soros' motive for wishing to legalize all drugs, like many of his motives, is opaque. But he unquestionably had no intention of seeing only marijuana legalized, let alone legalized only for medical purposes. While he is coy about answering questions about his own views on drug consumption, Soros' Drug Policy Alliance works for full legalization of all hard drugs, with no exceptions.

From the outset, Prop 215 was a Trojan horse. Its model of legalizing marijuana for medical purposes, then crafting the broadest possible definition of medical use, then moving for full legalization of the drug once "medical use" became a cynically meaningless distinction has been replicated in dozens of other states.

After Prop 215 became law, the acquisition of a "medical marijuana card" entitling its bearer to possess banned substances held the appeal of both violating the norms of social order and virtuously asserting one's rights in the face of government oppression: it was also easy to access, as "pill mill" type doctors provided the card to virtually anyone for a one-time payment of $100 or $200 and a claim of anxiety, or sleeplessness, or back pain, or some other vague illness.

Reports over the years place the percentage of medical marijuana cardholders who actually have cancer at only 4% of the total number of people possessing such cards, and the number of "dispensaries" that act as the "caregivers" envisioned by the law famously exceeds the number of Starbucks shops in states like California.

By 2016, the sheer size of the medical marijuana industry in California was massive, with only 5% of its output used for legal purposes for people with any medical ailment. And within that 5%, the percentage of severely ill people such as cancer and hospice patients, is vanishingly small:

> In 2016, the state produced an estimated 13.5 million pounds of pot, and 80 percent was illegally shipped out of state, according to a report prepared for the state by ERA Economics, an environmental and agricultural consulting firm. Of the remaining 20 percent,

only a quarter was sold legally for medicinal purposes.[143]

Such numbers breed cynicism towards both the medical industry and law enforcement: the healthy mother who goes to a storefront doctor and pays for a medical marijuana card in order to imbibe in recreational drugs is teaching her children how to participate in public corruption, among other things. And the quasi-mystical insistence that marijuana is a miracle drug that treats virtually any ailment, psychological or physical, leads to a culture where even pregnant women and professional athletes can talk themselves into believing that they are medicating, not harming their bodies by consuming pot.

In practice, legalizing marijuana for medical purposes in California led to de-facto full legalization. But, despite laxly enforced laws allowing medical marijuana for ailments ranging from insomnia to PMS to headaches, and despite 95% of the California crop being distributed illegally within the state or in other states, the drug legalization lobby subsidized by George Soros demanded even more leniency. They pushed for full legalization of marijuana in 2010 under Proposition 19, which surprisingly failed and again in 2016 with Proposition 64, which passed by a wide margin, 57% to 43%.

It took California 20 years to get from partial legalization of marijuana for medical purposes to full legalization for recreational use. In Washington (state), the same legislative steps took 14 years; in

Colorado, it took 12. It will doubtlessly take less time in other states now that the legalizers have mapped a political course and perfected their messaging. Even politically conservative states and elected officials are on board with legalizing marijuana so long as it is first introduced as medical marijuana and presented to the public as a necessary medical treatment for a condition affecting a sympathetic patient group.

In California in 1996, that patient group was people with AIDS. In Georgia in 2015, the first patient group appealing for legalization of medical marijuana derivatives was children afflicted with a severe and untreatable form of epilepsy. In that conservative, southern state, the Republican governor and majority-Republican legislature proceeded cautiously, intending to approve medical marijuana only for a limited number of medical conditions that do not respond to conventional therapies. But once the legislature approved marijuana for some conditions, other patient advocates began lobbying to be added to that patient list.

Low-THC medical marijuana oil was legalized in Georgia in 2015 to treat a few severe ailments: seizure disorders (including epilepsy), cancer, Crohn's disease, Lou Gehrig's disease, mitochondrial disease, multiple sclerosis, Parkinson's disease, and sickle cell disease. In 2017, that list was expanded to include Alzheimer's, AIDS, autism, epidermolysis bullosa, neuropathy, and Tourette's syndrome. Terminal patients in hospice care were also granted access to the oil. Then in 2018, the governor signed a law dramatically expanding the list to include Post-

Traumatic Stress Disorder and chronic pain, which places Georgia's laws, within just three years, on track to meet California's trajectory to full legalization.

Soldiers with war-related PTSD today are to the drug legalization movement what AIDS patients were in the mid-1990's: a bellwether to broader legalization.

Medical marijuana laws as tools for drug legalization are endlessly fungible, needing only a sympathetic group victimized by disease to set the entire legalization advocacy machine in motion. The legalization movement is fungible enough to even promote marijuana as a medical treatment for opioid addiction, playing up public concerns about the over-prescription of pharmaceutical drugs and hatred of "Big Pharma." In addition to advocating for medical marijuana for soldiers with PTSD, some veterans' groups are appealing for legalized marijuana to treat veterans addicted to opioids.

Roping in Conservatives

The current emphasis on aiding veterans also makes it easier for conservative legislators to justify their support for legal marijuana. Libertarians such as former Georgia Congressman Bob Barr have long been involved in drug legalization advocacy, but in recent years, even mainstream Republicans have joined forces with George Soros, either through their shared antipathy towards incarceration and the so-called War on Drugs or for even more mercenary motives. Former Secretary of State under Reagan, George P. Schultz is an outspoken member of the

Soros-funded Global Commission on Drug Policy, which has called for complete legalization of all drugs in all nations. The ACLU and the Koch brothers are jointly funding drug legalization efforts under the guise of criminal justice reform, with the Kochs fiscally rewarding conservative organizations, pundits and politicians that submit to their drug legalization agenda.

Former Republican Speaker of the House John Boehner, until recently an alleged hard opponent of marijuana legalization, is now looking to cash in on marijuana legalization through his new affiliation with Acerage Holdings, a multi-state marijuana manufacturing corporation. Echoing Obama, and using the newly politically correct term for marijuana, Boehner said in April that his "thinking on cannabis has evolved."[144] The Soros-funded Marijuana Policy Project employs a Director of Conservative Outreach, Don Murphy, who also recruited Senator Lindsey Graham to sponsor a medical marijuana bill in the Senate.[145]

Potentially life-saving, low-THC (non-psychotropic) marijuana extract oil that treats epilepsy in severely ill children might be called the gateway legislation that draws many politicians into the orbit of the marijuana legalization lobby. Add bipartisanship to the strengths of a marijuana legalization movement that now has a forty-year track record of achieving full legalization of the drug following its first steps anywhere towards limited treatment of chronically ill patients. In all cases, legalizing marijuana is merely their first step.

The path to legalization for even harder drugs such as heroin, cocaine, and methamphetamine is now being quietly constructed by MAPS, the Drug Policy Alliance, the Marijuana Policy Project, and NORML through what they are calling "harm reduction strategies." "Harm reduction" includes some small-scale activities such as setting up drug crisis medical care at music festivals, but the term also serves as a euphemism for the agenda of ending all drug prohibition laws. Although the leaders of these organizations variously deny they approve of full drug legalization or refuse to be pinned down on the topic, each organization also presents full legalization as the "cure" to the "worse problems" caused by criminalization of any drugs.

And each organization claims the mantle of "science" to combat the "ignorance of drug myths." Much of the purported science they cite is merely strategic rehashing of complaints about sentence differentials for crack or power cocaine, or criticism of Nancy Reagan's *Just Say No* advertising campaign – partisan public policy disagreements framed as scientific disputes. For example, among the Drug Policy Alliance's justifications for reconsidering cocaine's harmfulness is the argument that public health officials once may have exaggerated the potential prevalence and long-term effects of prenatal crack use on unborn infants. The DPA also justifies cocaine use by claiming that many of the negative life outcomes attributed to cocaine addiction are actually caused by poverty, not drugs: "Research now indicates that other factors, such as poverty, are responsible for many of the ills previously thought to be associated with cocaine and crack cocaine use," reads their website.[146]

Dr. Carl Hart, a professor of neuroscience and psychology at Columbia University, is one of the drug legalizers' favorite research scientists. Dr. Hart advocates for full legalization of all drugs on the grounds that drug laws are racist and that even prolific users of drugs like methamphetamine and crack cocaine should not be considered addicts if their use does not – by measurements he invented -- interfere with their ability to live what he terms productive lives. The clinical research Hart cites most frequently claims to debunk the addictive power of crack cocaine by showing that crack users will temporarily delay their next opportunity to ingest the drug – even for a few minutes at a time – if offered some financial reward for the time delay.

Such taxpayer-funded exercises in absurdity, along with endless accusations of racism, comprise much of what passes for scientific, pro-legalization addiction research in the universities. But its political power should not be underestimated in the current climate of growing support for mass legalization of drugs.

Curiously, Dr. Hart has a point when he observes that the vast amount of media attention and financial resources currently being poured into legalization of psychedelics demonstrates a bias against poor and minority drug users who choose other methods of getting high:

> One of the things that bothers me about the psychedelic movement … [they say] I'm

using this to go on a higher plane, or for some other reason, as opposed to the person on the corner who's getting high. You can rationalize your drug use however you want, but you're using drugs, and it's all the same thing. Even the marijuana smokers, when they talk about marijuana and not talk about crack, and not talk about heroin ... it's hypocrisy. It's ... elitism.[147]

Obama himself may have reached a similar conclusion about the elitism of the marijuana legalization movement based on the grim life story of the man who sold him drugs when he was a youth. Drug dealer Raymond Boyer was murdered by his lover, a young gay prostitute, a few years after Obama left Hawaii. The man who killed Boyer reported being abused by him. Both Boyer and his murderer were the sorts of addicts who did not escape, as Obama did, to college, career, and a stable life. Perhaps this story helps explain Obama's reluctance to enthusiastically endorse legalizing the drug.[148]

But it is Dr. Hart's vision of a world where all drugs are not only legal but also as socially accepted as alcohol that represents the accurate trajectory of the drug legalization movement. Full legalization is the stated goal of the billionaires funding the movement, including George Soros and those involved with the Global Commission on Drug Policy, and as such it needs to be considered seriously.

At this cultural moment, with full legalization of marijuana approaching and legalization of other drugs on the near horizon, it is important to understand the conditions that set the stage for such dramatic social change. Exploration of LSD began in the 1950's in universities as a movement focusing on consciousness, the mind, and spirituality. It was both a medical movement and a religious movement, but the religious aspects involved debunking and displacing other religious experiences, literally, and replacing them with drug experiences.

This aspect of the psychedelic revolution is frequently viewed as a relic of the counterculture of the Sixties. But in recent decades, new evangelists of psychedelic spirituality have attracted a new generation of followers willing to believe that they have found the real key to mystical experience itself – and additionally a perfect fusion of science and religion – through chemically altering their brains with psychedelic drugs.

Timothy Leary is generally considered the godfather of this phenomenon, but Leary quickly made himself an outcast in academic settings while the flame for replacing religion with psychedelic experiences burned on. Others of his peers – Ram Dass, Andrew Weil, and the religious history interpreter Huston Smith continued Leary's (actually meager) academic output to compose a philosophical or psychological treatise, more than a scientific theory, that psychedelic use provided access to higher levels of consciousness that would eventually eliminate destructive human tendencies such a nationalism, patriotism, war conflicts, prejudice, and even individual ego itself.

Two decades later, after the original wave of psychedelic research fell casualty to often-catastrophic recreational psychedelic use in the streets, Rick Doblin, founder of MAPS, and other psychedelic researchers set out to reincarnate this belief system simultaneously with their medical research efforts to test MDMA (Ecstasy, or Methylenedioxymethamphetamine) as a psychiatric treatment for PTSD experienced by war veterans and crime victims.

MAPS' MDMA research to treat PTSD would seem to have insurmountable design flaws: how would one create a control group that could not tell they weren't being given MDMA, or high enough doses of MDMA, as part of their therapy? Also, with miniscule test groups and participants self-selected to be willing to ingest powerful psychedelic drugs, it is difficult to believe MAPS did not recruit subjects who were already motivated to claim that the drugs helped them cure self-reported psychological problems. Such research flaws may become evident as MAPS' PTSD theories are subjected to Stage III clinical trials, which differ dramatically in size and scientific quality from the small-scale testing that characterizes Stage II experiments.

But whatever the outcome of the Stage III clinical trials, the results are unlikely to dampen the faith of the growing numbers of people who believe that psychedelics hold the key to human evolution and planetary sustainability itself. Rick Doblin and other practitioners of psychedelic therapeutic research believe that, looking forward, such drugs contain within them the potential to end prejudice, chauvinism, nationalism, and other ostensibly negative behaviors. They believe quite seriously that psychedelic use is the key to ushering in a world with no wars and no national boundaries, run by the United Nations rather than nation-states. In one 2016 interview, as Doblin was working with the Department of Defense on Phase III PTSD studies, he spoke openly about these ideas:

> Our mind, our intellect was squashed by the church, by religion, by fundamentalism … there was kind of a truce for 400 or 500 years of religion staying out of science and science staying out of religion but now that's even coming together so there's tremendous scientific research ... under the influence of psychedelics, people can have these unitive (sic) mystical experiences that connect us up with billions of years of history and thousands and thousands of years of human evolution.[149]

The United Nations, Doblin says, is the institution through which we may transcend:

> For me this was confirmed in 1984 when I got in touch with someone named Robert Muller who was the Assistant Secretary General of the United Nations and he'd written this book called *New Genesis Shaping of Global Spirituality* and his basic idea was

that we have United Nations to mediate disputed between cultures and if you look more closely a lot of those disputes are religious disputes. We need to get the mystics together to build this sense of alliance and for people to have a global spirituality, which doesn't mean one world religion.[150]

Doblin equates psychedelic use with tolerance, anti-racism, anti-Abrahamic faiths, and anti-nationalism:

We find that the religions that are more mystically based are more tolerant … Mysticism is an antidote to fundamentalism … Really, it's about integrating psychedelics … where I think people can have a deeper sense of meaning, a deeper sense of purpose, more tolerance, an antidote to prejudice of all sorts and so I think given all the crises that we face as a nation, as a culture, as a world, as a planetary species, I think psychedelics can play a major role in grounding people into something deeper and helping us really deal with the ways we're all bumping up against each other.[151]

Many prominent proponents of psychedelics believe that religious belief itself, as expressed in the Abrahamic religions, is merely a misremembering of ecstatic states of psychedelic intoxication that literally caused humans' primate ancestors to develop brain functions that enabled them to evolve into thinking, intelligent homo sapiens. Proponents of this theory include prominent anthropologists and ethnobiologists as well as physical scientists. It is their scientific credentials that appear to be convincing significant numbers of otherwise agnostic or atheistic opinion leaders to entertain the theological aspects of the theories they espouse – a theology in which the psychedelic drugs themselves are the spiritual entity at the center of the cosmology of their belief.

Several well-known researchers, some in universities, assert this "God Molecule" theory of DMT or LSD or Ayahuasca, including archeologist John Marco Allegro, chemist (and inventor of MDMA) Alexander Shulgin, neuroscientist John Lilly, psychologist Ralph Metzner, psychiatrist and psychopharmacologist Rick Strassman (author of *DMT: The Spirit Molecule*), Gerald Rubin Sandoval Issac, and ethnobotanist Terence McKenna. In 1970, Allegro published *The Sacred Mushroom and the Cross*, arguing that pre-Christian fertility cults in congress with psychedelic mushrooms conceived of the figure of Christ.

These men generally believe that through using psychedelics, mankind can finally shed the superstitious beliefs of the Abrahamic religions (Christianity, Judaism, and Islam) and evolve to a higher level of universal human consciousness ruled by both science and psychedelic spirituality.

Mandatory Madness

The suspicion by many in mainstream America that the drug legalization movement is something more than just a movement to dismantle the prison system and allow adults the freedom to ingest whatever substances they choose will find evidence in the philosophy expounded by the psychedelic evangelists. This raises a question: if a critical mass of people with power in the academic sciences believe that psychedelics are the only path to creating better, more tolerant, less war-like humans, how long will ingestion of such substances remain voluntary?

This question was posed by Aldous Huxley in 1932 in *Brave New World*, where the residents of a future dystopia numbed their resistance to totalitarian government control by obliterating their intellects and ego drives through near-continuous ingestion of Soma, a drug designed to satisfy sexual and emotional desires while rendering the consumer complacent to their lack of free will. In one of the most horrifying episodes of life imitating art, Huxley himself descended into a state of increasingly incontinent dependence on psychedelic drugs at the end of his life.

It may seem paranoid to suggest that the psychedelic legalization movement possess the power, or even the desire to force such drugs on the population at large. But by their own words, they do. Human evolution – and planetary healing – depends on it.

And there is no reason to believe they lack the resources as they plan, according to Rick Doblin, to set up a network of psychedelic drug clinics nationwide, modeled on hospice networks, where not only dying and ill people but also anyone seeking to "transcend" their moral and psychological crises may "evolve" to a higher state of humanity through experiences with psychedelics. After all, if was only a few years ago that the idea of marijuana legalization in all the fifty states seemed unlikely, but we are certainly on that path now.

# Endnotes

[1] http://nymag.com/daily/intelligencer/2018/05/obamas-legacy-has-already-been-destroyed.html

[2] Davis wrote a pornographic novel, *Sex Rebel; Black,* that was autobiographical and disclosed that he had sex with children. One chapter concerns the seduction by Davis and his first wife of a 13-year-old girl called Anne.

[3] The Obama administration had asserted that Title IX of the Education Amendments of 1972, which bans sex discrimination in public schools, also banned transgender discrimination. It sent a joint letter from the Departments of Education and Justice stating that students who identify as transgender must be allowed to use the private facilities that match their gender identity with "no medical diagnosis or treatment requirement."

[4] ASI published *Blood on His Hands: The True Story of Edward Snowden,* examining the disclosures from the former CIA and NSA employee that have put America and its allies in danger of further Russian aggression, Islamic terrorism, and Chinese cyber warfare.

[5] http://nymag.com/daily/intelligencer/2017/09/yes-im-dependent-on-weed.html

[6] https://www.omicsonline.org/open-access/marijuana-violence-and-law-2155-6105-S11-014.pdf

[7] Kushner is the husband to Ivanka Trump, son-in-law to President Donald Trump, and senior White House adviser. He is part owner of the real estate startup Cadre with George Soros and others.

[8] See the website www.silentpoison.com

[9] https://financialservices.house.gov/uploadedfiles/07072016_oi_t btj_sr.pdf

[10] See "The secret backstory of how Obama let Hezbollah off the hook. An ambitious U.S. task force targeting Hezbollah's billion-dollar criminal enterprise ran headlong into the White House's desire for a nuclear deal with Iran." https://www.politico.com/interactives/2017/obama-hezbollah-drug-trafficking-investigation/

[11] https://www.dni.gov/index.php/newsroom/press-

releases/press-releases-2016/item/1599-dni-clapper-fbi-director-comey-and-dia-director-stewart-to-salute-lgbtspies-at-2016icpride-summit

[12] https://www.justice.gov/opa/press-release/file/941551/download

[13] https://www.state.gov/r/remarks/2018/279593.htm

[14] https://americanmilitarynews.com/2017/10/exclusive-former-west-point-professors-letter-exposes-corruption-cheating-and-failing-standards-full-letter/

[15] https://english.hebbel-am-ufer.de/media-center/texts/vitamin-b-bini-adamczak/

[16] http://foreignpolicy.com/2013/03/26/gay-in-the-ussr/

[17] "Building a Better World for Transpeople: Reed Erickson and the Erickson Educational Foundation," International Journal of Transgenderism, Aaron Devor and Nicolas Matte, October 15, 2008.

[18] Koch, Stephen: *Double Lives. Spies and Writers in the Secret War of Ideas Against the West,* (The Free Press, New York, 1994), page 186.

[19]

https://www.telegraph.co.uk/culture/books/3638752/Bloomsburys-final-secret.html

[20] Dr. Paul Kengor writes in *The American Spectator* that, "The ugly truth, however, is that American communists have been after the Boy Scouts for over a century. Marxists were hellbent on taking down the Boy Scouts prior to even the Bolsheviks taking down czarist Russia." See  https://spectator.org/the-marxist-progressive-war-on-the-boy-scouts/

[21]

http://press.vatican.va/content/salastampa/en/bollettino/pubblico/2017/10/05/171005d.html

[22] http://wmst.umd.edu/dcqs18

[23] http://www.sexchangeregret.com/

[24] http://www.lgbtfunders.org/research/?transformational-impact-u-s-foundation-funding-trans-communities-2

[25] Our book, *Back from the Dead: The Return of the Evil Empire,* exposes how the fall of the Berlin Wall misled many into thinking the Soviet KGB was dead. But infiltration of the West continued through "cultural Marxism," and penetration by

enemy agents, while the KGB, now called the FSB, looted Russia, consolidated its power, and rebuilt the Russian military, including its nuclear forces.

[26] Rather than embrace Christianity, the evidence shows Russia has embraced the Russian Orthodox Church, always a tool of Soviet intelligence.

[27] "Who Are the Rich, White Men Institutionalizing Transgender Ideology?" The Federalist (February 20, 2018).

[28] https://www.glaad.org/blog/arcus-and-novo-foundations-pledge-20-million-trans-organizations

[29] The Campden FB (formerly Families in Business) website reports, "Marmon Holdings, an international association that is owned by the Pritzker family and made up of more than 125 manufacturing and service businesses with combined revenues of $7 billion, is to sell 60% of its shares to Berkshire Hathaway, the conglomerate owned and managed by billionaire Warren Buffett for $4.5 billion."

[30] http://www.pbs.org/wnet/facesofamerica/video/islam-and-identity/140/

[31] A Citizenship in the World merit badge was established by the Boy Scouts in 1992.

[32] Romans 1:26-27 Because of this God abandoned them to dishonorable passions, for their women exchanged the natural relationship, for the relationship which is against nature; and so did the men, for they gave up the natural relationship with women, and were inflamed with their desire for each other, and men were guilty of shameful conduct with men. So within themselves they received their due and necessary rewards for their error.

[33] https://www.justice.gov/opa/pr/ira-isaacs-sentenced-48-months-prison-los-angeles-adult-obscenity-case

[34] The Stop Enabling Sex Traffickers Act (SESTA) and Allow States and Victims to Fight Online Sex Trafficking Act (FOSTA)

[35] https://www.congress.gov/congressional-record/2013/12/09/extensions-of-remarks-section/article/E1811-1

[36] www.TrevorLoudon.com

[37] https://nypost.com/2018/05/26/campaign-contributor-helped-

obamas-score-netflix-deal/

38
https://www.americanthinker.com/blog/2018/05/federal_lawsuit_accuses_obama_presidential_center_of_bait_and_switch_in_land_grab_of_park_space.html

39 https://news.kochind.com/news/2018/keep-local-marijuana-laws-from-going-up-in-smoke

40 https://www.wsj.com/articles/trump-adviser-jared-kushner-didnt-disclose-startup-stake-1493717405

41 The signers were Lieutenant Colonel David L. Sonnier, US Army (Retired); Michael J. Matt, editor of *The Remnant*: Christopher A. Ferrara, author, attorney, and president of the American Catholic Lawyers Association, Inc.; Chris Jackson, Catholics4Trump.com; and, Elizabeth Yore, Esq., Founder of YoreChildren.

42 http://americasurvival.org/2017/02/catholics-ask-trump-to-probe-soros-obama-clinton-conspiracy-at-vatican.html#axzz5HBfH3PrF

43 Judi McLeod of *Canada Free Press* documented how Obama planned the "fundamental transformation" of Canada by taking down Stephen Harper's government.

44 Kitty Kelley, Oprah, page 428, Kindle location 8410.

45 See, for example, Wikipedia article on Oprah Winfrey, date referenced 05-07-2018, https://en.wikipedia.org/wiki/Oprah_Winfrey.

46 https://www.youtube.com/watch?v=KMsGfVvxPwY KITTY KELLEY INTERVIEW – Here Kitty Kelley says that Oprah may be the world's most powerful woman. This was contemporaneous with the release of her unauthorized biography (2010).

47 http://makinggayhistory.com/podcast/greg-brock/

48 Kitty Kelley, *Oprah,* p. 494.

49 I personally discussed the dynamics of this situation on America's Survival. http://americasurvival.org/2015/08/is-bernie-sanders-the-new-age-messiah.html#axzz5EbTkY0m7 or https://tinyurl.com/ybl6bfle.

50 https://www.barnesandnoble.com/readouts/stealing-fire-how-silicon-valley-the-navy-seals-and-maverick-scientists-are-revolutionizing-the-way-we-live-and-work/

[51] The Reverend Sun Myung Moon, founder of *The Washington Times*, was one of several figures claiming to be the Messiah. He claimed to have succeeded where Jesus Christ failed and predicted a one-world global religion. Though touted as an anti-communist, Moon received a "Universal Peace Award" at the U.N., called for a U.N.-based religious body, and declared, "As long as America sticks with its nationalistic pride it will never be able to embrace the world." Moon even conducted one of his many notorious "mass weddings" at the United Nations itself on January 27, 2001.

[52] Peter LeMesurier, *The Armageddon Script*, page 237.

[53] The Acknowledgments to *The Armageddon Script* give credit to Findhorn's Thule Press for allowing him to quote from his forthcoming book then due in 1982, *The Cosmic Eye.*

[54] Marilyn Ferguson, *The Aquarian Conspiracy,* (1980 edition), page 216. As for Jim Jones and his People's Temple, see the 1972 and 1973 editions of Spiritual Community Guide (there may be more, but those are in my personal library) list of New Age centers, page 25 of 1972 edition, "People's Temple – Jim Jones). The Jonestown massacre occurred in Guyana in 1978.

[55] I pulled this astonishing speech down pre-Google on the then Alta Vista search engine on March 21, 1999. I didn't take Solana's word alone for it. I then located Madeline Albright's State Department page where she said "Solana has the power and has had it since January 30th. We are speaking with one voice through Javier Solana." Kofi Annan's book also testifies to it. See *Kofi Annan – Interventions* (2012), pages 98-100.

[56]

https://www.satrakshita.com/nieves_matthews_sannyas_account .htm. Also https://www.satrakshita.com/nieves_matthews_interview.htm. Nieves was Salvador de Madariaga's oldest daughter. Her guru of choice was Bhagwan Shree Rajneesh, aka "OSHO". In this interview, she tells of her family's connections to Sufism, Krishnamurti, etc.

[57] There is no shortage of books regarding Krishnamurti and the New Age campaign for his acceptance that began in 1920 and culminated in large Holland based campfires at Camp Ommen in the Netherlands. Camp Ommen's grounds and the castle in

which Krishnamurti lived while in Holland was donated by a major figure in the early days of Boy Scouting, Lord Philip van Pallandt. https://en.wikipedia.org/wiki/Philip_van_Pallandt
[58] http://www.sai-maa.com/en/about-sai-maa
[59]

http://www.cnn.com/2011/CRIME/03/14/ray.sweat.lodge.witnesses/index.html
[60]

https://en.wikipedia.org/wiki/Heaven%27s_Gate_(religious_group)
[61]

http://www.nbcnews.com/id/42711922/ns/technology_and_science-science/t/earth-day-co-founder-killed-composted-girlfriend/#.WwwlA-4vzX4
[62] http://www.nxivm.com/
[63]

https://rhga.ru/science/center/ezo/publications/The_Occult_Revival.pdf
[64] "The Color Purple" was a 1985 movie based on a novel by Alice Walker. It had won major literary prizes (Pulitzer and National Award for Fiction). It was the story of a young girl abused by her father and placed in an early unloved marriage where she suffered more abuse. Unfortunately, the story line was that her "salvation" was by her husband's mistress who also conducted a lesbian relationship with the heroine of the story.
[65] http://www.oprah.com/health_wellness/high-tea-parties-everything-you-need-to-know
[66] Kitty Kelley, *Oprah,* page 340.
[67] http://www.oprah.com/inspiration/silas-musick-activist
[68] http://www.citizensproject.org/2017/03/21/support-banning-conversion-therapy-co-house-bill-1156/
[69] The history of Oprah's early years with the loving family in Kosciusko, her years in Milwaukee with her mother Vernita, and her high school and college years are well laid out in Kitty Kelley's comprehensive "unauthorized" biography of Oprah.
[70] Oprah, op. cit.,
[71] This is an encapsulated video presentation of Oprah's life, sympathetic to Oprah and her various New Age, "spiritual," pro-gay promotions. It is about 5 minutes of watching.

https://www.youtube.com/watch?v=cGf85-bQmEQ

[72] Kitty Kelley, Oprah, page 5.

[73] Kitty Kelley Oprah, A biography, page 5, Kindle location 223, 225; page 16, Kindle location 425, 432.

[74] See, for example, this posted web article http://gawker.com/5774540/oprah-fired-me-for-talking-about-jesus.

[75] http://www.chicagonow.com/the-life-and-times-of-a-young-republican/2011/03/oprah-fired-me-for-talking-about-jesus-claims-cousin/;

[76] Kitty Kelley's book Oprah is available both in print and as a Kindle edition contains extensive discussions of Oprah's family's expressions of dismay over her rejection of Jesus and adoption of New Age beliefs. (Pages 343, Kindle location 6696).

[77] Kitty Kelley, Oprah, page 34 – interview with Aunt Katharine.

[78] Orpah was the sister of Ruth (Ruth 1:4, KJV). The explanation for "Oprah" rather than "Orpah" was that the name was often mispronounced, and the mispronunciation stuck.

[79] Marilyn Ferguson's appearance on her program appeared to be a major shift to New Age philosophical type programming in preference to her human sexual crisis-type themes that heavily characterized earlier programming.

[80] Oprah, page 142, Kindle location 2802.

[81] New Age Politics, Mark Satin, page 289.

[82] Oprah's Aunt Katharine Carr Esters was emphatic that Oprah had been untruthful, even "lied." She said, per Kitty Kelley's biographical work, that Oprah admitted to her that she lied because "that's what people want to hear." Kelley, op. cited, page 20, Kindle location 493.

[83] Jeremiah 10:23 (King James Version).

[84] Jeremiah 10:24. Supra.

[85] Jonathan Rauch, Brookings Institution op-ed, "Why gay rights may be President Obama's biggest legacy," May 11, 2012; https://www.brookings.edu/opinions/why-gay-rights-may-be-president-obamas-biggest-legacy/

[86] See the Victory Institute's list of Obama's LGBTQ appointments: https://victoryinstitute.org/programs/presidential-appointments-initiative/lgbt-appointments-obama-biden-administration/

[87] Juliet Eilperin, *Washington Post*, "For Obama Rainbow White House was a moment worth savoring," June 30, 2015; https://www.washingtonpost.com/news/post-politics/wp/2015/06/30/for-obama-rainbow-white-house-was-a-moment-worth-savoring/

[88] WHEC.com: "News or Noise: Did Pres. Obama refuse to honor officers with lighting," May 17, 2017; http://www.whec.com/news/president-obama-white-house-lighting/4487890/

[89] David J. Garrow, *Rising Star: The Making of Barack Obama*, (William Morrow, an imprint of HarperCollins, 2017), p. 65 (nanny) and pp. 69-72 (Frank Marshall Davis)

[90] UK Daily Mail, "Obama's sex secrets laid bare..."; May 3, 2017; http://www.dailymail.co.uk/news/article-4470040/Obama-s-sex-drugs-past-laid-bare-new-biography.html#ixzz5EzT9T3ae

[91] Jamie Weinstein podcast with David Garrow, circa May 2017: https://soundcloud.com/jamieweinstein/david-garrow

[92] Garrow, *Rising Star*, p. 113.

[93] Weinstein podcast interview with Garrow, around the 56-min. mark.

[94] CSPAN interview with Garrow by Brian Lamb, Part One, May 12, 2017; https://www.c-span.org/video/?428424-2/qa-david-garrow-part-1.

[95] See David Garrow's website, including "The Strategy," http://www.davidgarrow.com/File/DJG2012TNRCarpenter.pdf

[96] See J.L. King's book, *On the Down Low: A Journey into the Lives of 'Straight' Black Men Who Sleep with Men*, (Broadway Books, 2004).

[97] Dr. Joseph and Linda Ames Nicolosi, *A Parent's Guide to Preventing Homosexuality*, (InterVarsity Press: 2002), p. 22.

[98] Garrow, *Rising Star*.

[99] Michelle Gallardo, "Choir director found murdered," Dec. 24, 2007, ABC7 Chicago, http://abc7chicago.com/archive/5854125/

[100] Jerome Corsi, WND.com, "Trinity Church member reveal Obama shocker: Matchmaker Rev. Jeremiah Wright "provided cover for gays"; Oct. 2, 2012; http://www.wnd.com/2012/10/trinity-church-members-reveal-obama-shocker/

[101] Jerome Corsi, WND.com, "Claim: Obama hid 'gay life' to

become president," September 11, 2012;
http://www.wnd.com/2012/09/claim-obama-hid-gay-life-to-become-president/

[102] Bill Daley, *Chicago Tribune,* "Man's County, Chicago's oldest gay bathhouse, closing after 44 years," Dec. 30, 2017; http://www.chicagotribune.com/lifestyles/ct-life-mans-country-bathhouse-closing-1230-story.html

[103] Ben Smith, Politico.com, "Obama accuser has long rap sheet," June 18, 2008; https://www.politico.com/story/2008/06/obama-accuser-has-long-rap-sheet-011164

[104] George Maschke, "WhiteHouse.com's polygraph examination of Larry Sinclair," AntiPolygraph YouTube channel, June 17, 2008: https://www.youtube.com/watch?v=Hc8Ys8iXTiU.

[105] See Sinclair's book, *Barack Obama and Larry Sinclair: Cocaine, Sex, Lies & Murder?*; available on Kindle after being republished by Movie Skool LLC.

[106] Robert Donachie, "Dude Who Claimed Sex With Obama Is Livid At Media's Obsession With Stormy Daniels," Daily Caller, March 23, 2018; http://dailycaller.com/2018/03/23/larry-sinclair-obama-media-stormy-daniels/

[107] See Paul Kengor's book, *The Communist: Frank Marshall Davis: The Untold Story of Barack Obama's Mentor* (Simon & Schuster: 2012).

[108] *Windy City Times*, "Letter: Obama on Marriage," Feb. 11, 2004; http://www.windycitymediagroup.com/lgbt/Letters-Obama-on-Marriage-Gay-Games/4018.html

[109] *Windy City Times*, "Obama once backed full gay marriage"; Jan. 13, 2009, http://www.windycitymediagroup.com/lgbt/Obama-once-backed-full-gay-marriage/20229.html

[110] Tracy Baim, *Obama and the Gays: A Political Marriage* (Prairie Avenue Productions: 2010), location 1004 on Kindle version.

[111] Vote Smart, full transcript Saddleback Presidential Forum: https://votesmart.org/public-statement/658545/full-transcript-saddlcback-presidential-forum-sen-barack-obama-john-mccain-moderated-by-rick-warren/

[112] Baim, "Obama and the Gays," Kindle version, location 2019.

[113] CBS: Obama administration will no longer defend DOMA":
https://www.cbsnews.com/news/obama-administration-will-no-longer-defend-doma/

[114] Wikipedia, "List of U.S. state constitutional amendments banning same-sex unions by type";
https://en.wikipedia.org/wiki/List_of_U.S._state_constitutional_amendments_banning_same-sex_unions_by_type

[115] David Axelrod, "Believer: My 40 Years in Politics, (Penguin Press: 2015), p. 447.

[116] Josh Lederman, AP, "Logtime aide says Obama misled on gay marriage opposition"; Feb. 10, 2015;
https://apnews.com/8dc24e8cbad74e359e839c242b2582a4/longtime-aide-says-obama-misled-gay-marriage-opposition

[117] David Maraniss, *Barack Obama: The Story* (Simon &Schuster), p. 217

[118] Robert Gagnon is the author of *The Bible and Homosexual Practice: Texts and Hermeneutics*. See his informative website, www.RobGagnon.net.

[119] Barack Obama, *Audacity of Hope: Thoughts on Reclaiming the American Dream* (Crown Publishers), p. 222.

[120] Author, RepublicansForMorality.com, "Theology expert says Obama grossly distorts Scriptures to support homosexual cause," Oct. 23, 2008;
https://republicansformorality.com/2008/10/23/theology-expert-says-obama-grossly-distorts-scriptures-to-support-homosexual-cause/

[121] Manya Brachear, *Chicago Tribune*, "Local reverend defends Obama on same-sex marriage," May 17, 2012;
http://www.chicagotribune.com/news/local/breaking/chi-local-reverend-defends-obama-on-samesex-marriage-20120517-story.html

[122] Ben Brumfield, "Voters approve same-sex marriage for the first time," CNN, Nov. 2, 2012;
https://www.cnn.com/2012/11/07/politics/pol-same-sex-marriage/index.html,

[123] See, for example, the Jack Phillips case currently before the U.S. Supreme Court; Phillips, a Christian cake maker, is defended by Alliance Defending Freedom:
http://www.adfmedia.org/news/prdetail/8700.

[124] Michael Shear, New York Times, "Obama Calls for End to 'Conversion' Therapies for Gay and Transgender Youth," April 8, 2015;
https://www.nytimes.com/2015/04/09/us/politics/obama-to-call-for-end-to-conversion-therapies-for-gay-and-transgender-youth.html

[125] Alliance Defending Freedom, 2015:
http://www.adfmedia.org/files/obamareligiousfreedomattacks.pdf

[126] https://www.justice.gov/archives/opa/blog/memorandum-selected-united-state-attorneys-investigations-and-prosecutions-states

[127]
https://www.justice.gov/sites/default/files/oip/legacy/2014/07/23/dag-guidance-2011-for-medical-marijuana-use.pdf

[128] https://www.rollingstone.com/politics/news/obamas-pot-breakthrough-20140305

[129] https://www.newyorker.com/magazine/2014/01/27/going-the-distance-david-remnick

[130] ibid.

[131] https://www.washingtonpost.com/world/national-security/obama-to-commute-hundreds-of-federal-drug-sentences-in-final-grants-of-clemency/2017/01/16/c99b4ba6-da5e-11e6-b8b2-cb5164beba6b_story.html?utm_term=.e0b83a233738

[132] https://www.nationalreview.com/2016/08/obama-releases-prisoners-guilty-gun-crimes/

[133] https://www.city-journal.org/html/decriminalization-delusion-14037.html

[134] https://www.rollingstone.com/politics/features/obama-on-his-legacy-trumps-win-and-the-path-forward-w452527

[135] https://www.nytimes.com/2018/04/20/well/move/runners-high-marijuana-pot-sports-exercise-weed.html

[136] https://www.nytimes.com/2017/02/20/health/marijuana-pregnancy-mothers.html?action=click&contentCollection=Health&module=RelatedCoverage&region=Marginalia&pgtype=article

[137] https://www.nytimes.com/2017/02/02/health/marijuana-and-pregnancy.html?action=click&contentCollection=Health&modu

le=RelatedCoverage&region=Marginalia&pgtype=article

[138] https://missionlocal.org/2010/09/local-marijuana-advocate-says-no-on-prop-19/

[139] Cliff Kincaid, *The Playboy Foundation: A Mirror of the Culture?* (Capital Research Center, Studies in Philanthropy #13, 1992), p. 47.

[140] https://www.drugpolicy.org/about-us#history-of-dpa

[141] https://www.washingtontimes.com/news/2014/apr/2/billionaire-george-soros-turns-cash-into-legalized/

[142] https://www.cnbc.com/id/36179727

[143] https://nypost.com/2018/01/01/recreational-marijuana-is-officially-legal-in-california/

[144] https://www.nytimes.com/2018/04/11/us/politics/boehner-cannabis-marijuana.html

[145] https://www.politico.com/magazine/story/2016/09/lindsey-graham-pot-journey-medical-marijuana-214266

[146] http://www.drugpolicy.org/drug-facts/cocaine-and-crack-facts

[147] https://www.youtube.com/watch?v=SMsquUcea-E&t=6364s, conversation at 1:18 minutes.

[148] http://www.dailymail.co.uk/news/article-2547667/EXCLUSIVE-Obamas-high-school-pot-dealer-future-president-thanked-good-times-yearbook-beaten-death-gay-lover-fights-flatulence-drugs.html

[149] https://www.youtube.com/watch?v=MHSFGeJaf6Q, conversation at 1:30 minutes.

[150] Ibid.

[151] Ibid.